calgary
city of animals

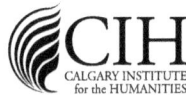

Calgary Institute for the Humanities Series
Co-published with the Calgary Institute for the Humanities
ISSN 2560-6883 (Print) ISSN 2560-6891 (Online)

The humanities help us to understand who we are and where we came from; they help us to understand and respect-fully engage with those who are different from us; and they encourage a curiosity and imagination that allows us to bring older ideas to the new worlds in which we find ourselves. Books in this series embody this spirit of inquiry.

No. 1 **Calgary: City of Animals** edited by Jim Ellis

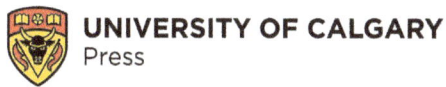
UNIVERSITY OF CALGARY
Press

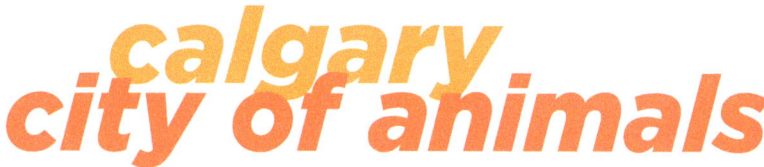
calgary
city of animals

edited by jim ellis

a special publication of **the university of calgary press**
in co-operation with **the calgary institute for the humanities**

CALGARY INSTITUTE FOR THE HUMANITIES SERIES
ISSN 2560-6883 (Print)   ISSN 2560-6891 (Online)

University of Calgary Press
2500 University Drive NW
Calgary, Alberta
Canada T2N 1N4

press.ucalgary.ca

Library and Archives Canada Cataloguing in Publication

Calgary (2017)
      Calgary : city of animals / edited by Jim Ellis.

(Calgary Institute for the Humanities series)
Includes bibliographical references.
Issued in print and electronic formats.
Co-published by: Calgary Institute for the Humanities.
ISBN 978-1-55238-967-6 (softcover).--ISBN 978-1-55238-968-3 (Open Access PDF).
--ISBN 978-1-55238-969-0 (PDF).--ISBN 978-1-55238-970-6 (EPUB).
--ISBN 978-1-55238-971-3 (Kindle)

      1. Human-animal relationships--Alberta--Calgary. 2. Animals--Social aspects--
Alberta--Calgary. I. Ellis, Jim, 1964-, editor II. Calgary Institute for the Humanities
issuing body III. Title. IV. Series: Calgary Institute for the Humanities series.

QL85.C35 2017   591.97123'38   C2017-902549-X
                                             C2017-902550-3

The University of Calgary Press acknowledges the support of the Government of Alberta through the Alberta Media Fund for our publications. We acknowledge the financial support of the Government of Canada. We acknowledge the financial support of the Canada Council for the Arts for our publishing program.

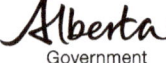 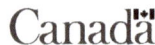

Front flap image: *Katie Daniothy sitting on a pig.* 1890–1905, Glenbow Archives, NC-39-302
Back flap image: *Aerial view showing helicopter transporting dinosaur replica to new prehistoric park at zoo, Calgary, Alberta.* 1985, Glenbow Archives, NA-5654-126a

Cover art: *Magpie* by Lisa Brawn
Cover design, page design, and typesetting by glenn mielke

photo: Andrea S. H. Hunt. Photo courtesy of the Calgary Wildlife Rehabilitation Society

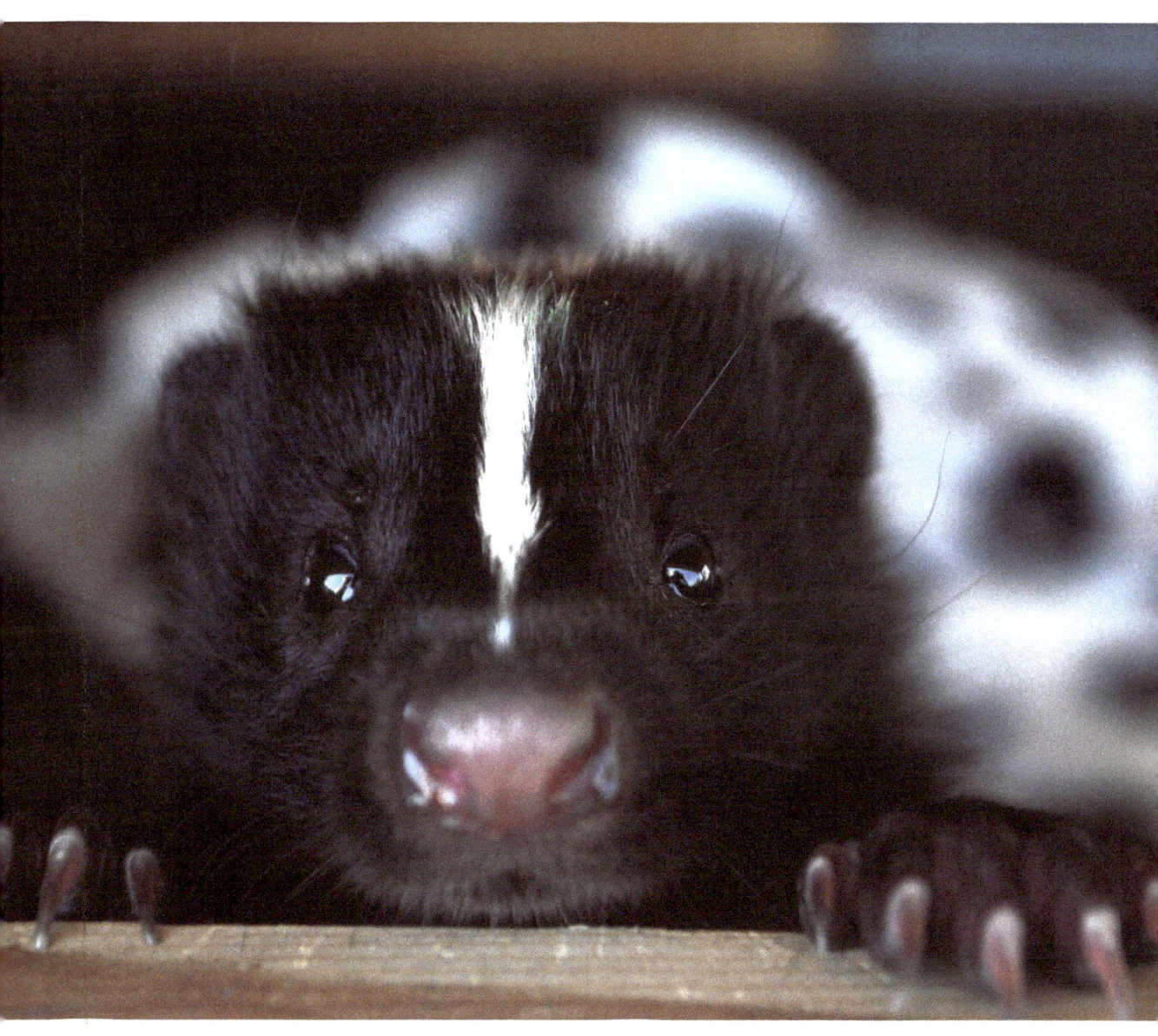

contents

acknowledgements   **ix**

introduction   **xi**
jim ellis, director, cih

how canadians used to live with livestock in cities   **1**
sean kheraj

outlaw horses & the true spirit of calgary   **10**
in the automobile age
susan nance

silence of the song dogs   **22**
shelley m. alexander

counting chickadees & reimagining the map of calgary   **32**
angela waldie

critical animal studies & the humanities: **42**
a critical introduction
mohammad sadeghi esfahlani

wild animals in the city   **56**
jenna mcfarland & andrea hunt, calgary wildlife rehabilitation society

light pollution in an animal city   **62**
maureen luchsinger & laura griffin, ann & sandy cross conservation area

66 excerpt from **our biodivercity**
calgary's 10-year biodiversity strategic plan

74 **squirrel vs. gopher**
from *calgary i love you, but you're killing me*
one yellow rabbit ensemble

76 **becoming insects** *a new universe*
kimberley cooper, artistic director, decidedly jazz danceworks

82 **kaleidoscopic animalia**
an exhibition designed and curated by paul hardy
paul hardy & melanie kjorlien

94 **lisa brawn interview & portfolio**
wild bird woodcuts
calgary institute for the humanities

104 **her dark materials:**
yvonne mullock's **dark horse** *at stride gallery*
jim ellis

114 **conclusion**
jim ellis

117 **notes**

122 **contributors**

acknowledgements

This book grew out of the Calgary Institute for the Humanities' Annual Community Seminar for 2016. The idea for the seminar emerged from the CIH's Advisory Board, which included Bill Dickson, Fran Jamison, JoAnn McCaig, Judy MacLachlan, Murray Laverty, Valerie Seaman, Nancy Tousley, Rod Wade and Lynn Willoughby. Many thanks are due for their guidance and support of the project from beginning to end.

At the CIH, Caroline Loewen and Moe Esfahlani provided research assistance and organizational support for the seminar.

At UCalgary Press, Brian Scrivener, Helen Hajnoczky, and Melina Cusano have been exceptionally supportive of the project and our vision for the book; thanks to Glenn Mielke for his patience and the beautiful design.

Sharla Mann did picture research, and provided administrative support for all stages of the book production with efficiency and good humor. Finally, I am grateful to the three original panelists of the seminar, as well as to all of the other contributors to the book, for being so cooperative and good humoured as we slowly shaped our idea of what the book should try to accomplish. I hope that the results reward their patience.

introduction
jim ellis
director, calgary institute for the humanities

Long before the traders and the North West Mounted Police and the European settlers arrived, and long before the peoples of the First Nations gathered at the place
called *Mohkínstsis*, there were the animals. From its beginnings as a human settlement
at the confluence of the Elbow and the Bow Rivers, the story of Calgary is not just a
history of people but, in many ways, the history of our dealings with our fellow creatures.
The fur trade, cattle ranching, and the Greatest Outdoor Show on Earth have all left profound marks on the city's culture and geography. How have our interactions with animals
shaped the city? What traces can we locate on Calgary's landscape, real or imaginary?

The story of human and animal relations is not just a story of the past. Our cohabitation
with animals also, of course, concerns the present, and the future too (we hope). According to the City of Calgary's biodiversity document, there are at present 52 species
of mammals in the city, 365 species of birds, 4 of reptiles, 6 of amphibians and 22
species of fish.[1] Where do these animals live in the city? How does the city support animal life? How do we categorize the different animals that live among us (pets, livestock,
entertainers, pests?), and how does this affect our relations with them? More radically,
what does it mean to think of humans as one animal among many in an urban biosphere? How can we make the city a site that supports the co-flourishing of all of its
animal life, human and non-human?

The contributions to this book come at these questions from a wide range of perspectives, including those of historians, geographers, artists, writers, animal welfare workers,
wildlife enthusiasts, and ordinary Calgarians, all of whom participated in the Calgary Institute for the Humanities' (CIH) Community Seminar in April 2016. Each year the CIH
explores a question of both timely and enduring relevance, and invites three scholars
from different fields to join a day-long conversation with the citizens of Calgary.
Founded in 1976, the CIH is Canada's oldest humanities institute, and for over thirty
years it has been engaging Calgarians in discussions of our common concerns. Of particular interest to the institute lately have been questions concerning our environment,
topics drawn from what are called the Environmental Humanities.

The title of the 2016 seminar, "Calgary: City of Animals," reflects our particular interest
in exploring our relation to the animals that live among us. Moderator Ken Lima-Coelho
guided seminar participants through the morning session, which featured presentations
from our three guest scholars. At lunch, each table of eight discussed a question posed
by one of our speakers. Sean Kheraj asked whether Canadians should be permitted to
practice livestock husbandry in cities. Susan Nance asked what kinds of working animals
still lived in the city, and whether animals should be expected to earn their keep in the
modern world. Shelley M. Alexander asked participants to consider what strategies are
necessary to ensure the co-flourishing of humans, pets, and urban wild animals such as
coyotes. The lunchtime discussions were moderated by members of the CIH's Advisory
Committee, who summarized the lively discussions for the afternoon session and posed
questions back to our speakers.

The seminar as a whole drew on the wide-ranging and interdisciplinary field of Animal
Studies. Western philosophy from the ancient Greeks onward has explored the question
of the animal, often using the animal to define what it is to be human. Renaissance
thinkers, for example, saw the human as suspended between animals and angels, par-
taking of both natures but striving to escape the former and ascend toward the latter.
Other philosophers, starting with Aristotle, posited the existence of three different kinds
of souls: vegetable, animal, and human, with the human containing all three. The key
difference between animals and humans, argued some philosophers, is the ability to use
language and reason, although writers such as Michel de Montaigne believed that animals might well have language that we just failed to understand. René Descartes
famously argued that because animals did not have language they could not have souls
and should therefore be considered to be essentially machines, a view that justified
whatever use humans might choose to make of them. Jeremy Bentham, responding to

Descartes, insisted that the important question was not whether animals could reason but whether they could suffer.

It is a renewed attention to the suffering of animals that fuels much contemporary work in Animal Studies. From the nineteenth century onward, philosophers and activists have argued in different ways for the rights of animals, whether these are as limited as the right to be treated humanely or as far-reaching as granting legal or political rights on a level with humans (this is not entirely unprecedented: animals were occasionally defendants in legal trials in the Middle Ages). Calgarians have been discussing these issues for many years now; as Susan Nance notes in her essay in this volume, the welfare of animals has been a topic in the local press almost since the Calgary Stampede started, back in 1912. But with our increasing concern with global climate change and habitat loss, the question has expanded beyond animal suffering to consider the possibilities for animal survival—including, of course, the human animal.

This book explores our relations with non-human animals in a variety of ways and in a variety of voices. The first group of essays contains the talks given at the seminar, as well as a couple of contributions by scholars who were in attendance. Susan Nance, a historian of animal entertainment, looks at the story of a horse called Greasy Sal who performed in the Calgary Stampede in the late 1920s. Nance follows one horse's career to illuminate what goes on "behind the stage" at animal entertainments but also to avoid the kind of generalizing about animals that often happens in histories of this kind. Here is the story of one particular animal, or at least as much as can be reconstructed from the archives. Shelley M. Alexander, a geographer who specializes in wild animals, particularly carnivores, highlights some of the contradictions inherent in our relations with animals in the city: we want to see them, but we want to see them on our own terms. When coyotes eat our garbage or our pets we get outraged, and often fail to take responsibility for our own actions. How can we rethink our relations to these predators, who are an important part of our urban biosphere? The essay by our third speaker at the seminar, historian Sean Kheraj, looks at a contemporary issue with a long past: the phenomenon of urban husbandry. Whereas now it is mostly urban hipsters who keep chickens or bees in the backyard, in Canadian cities in the nineteenth century, cows, pigs, sheep, and chickens were a common sight, and not just in backyards. Kheraj looks at when and why farm animals left the city.

Two other scholarly contributions come from two of the seminar attendees. Angela Waldie, a practitioner of ecocriticism, follows along with Calgarian naturalist Gus Yaki on his monthly Elbow River Bird Survey, a long-running example of citizen science. Yaki and his wife Aileen Pelzer have been guiding volunteer bird counts for over twenty years now, observing the changes to urban bird life and the urban landscape. Waldie shows how being more attentive to the animals among us can enrich and deepen our understanding of place. Mohammad Sadeghi Esfahlani, the project manager for the CIH's community seminar, discusses a particular outgrowth of animal studies called Critical Animal Studies, and assesses some of its key ideas. In particular, he discusses some ethical issues around eating animals (at the seminar, we had sandwiches for both carnivores and vegans).

These scholarly voices are complemented by contributions from some of the people who work with animals in the city. At the seminar, we had representatives from the Calgary Zoo, Calgary Parks, the Calgary Stampede, Canadian Parks and Wilderness Society, and Calgary River Valleys, among others. Jenna McFarland and Andrea Hunt, representatives of the Calgary Wildlife Rehabilitation Society, responded to our invitation to contribute a discussion of the work of their organization, and the kinds of animals they rescue and treat. A second essay by Maureen Luchsinger and Laura Griffin from the Ann and Sandy Cross Conservation Area addresses the importance of dark refuges for non-human animals. A sustainable habitat means more than just land; it also means preserving spaces of nocturnal darkness or, as Angela Waldie observes in her piece, enough quiet for birds to hear each other. To round out this section we include an excerpt from the City of Calgary's biodiversity strategy document, which illustrates what is guiding the city's thinking and planning over the next ten years, in order to sustain the various species that live in the urban biosphere.

The third major group of contributions to this book takes yet another approach, showing how artists in the city of Calgary have represented and responded to the animals that live among us. The anthropomorphic song from the One Yellow Rabbit ensemble's show *Calgary I Love You, But You're Killing Me* features three of Calgary's most familiar urban dwellers: gophers, squirrels, and magpies. Kimberley Cooper, the choreographer and artistic director of Decidedly Jazz Danceworks, talks about finding inspiration in insects and insect movement for her latest work, *A New Universe*. Cooper is known for her innovative approach to jazz dance, which involves "creaturizing" human movement; the strange hybrids of humans and bugs in her work challenge us to explore our communalities with other creaturely worlds. Internationally known fashion designer and Calgarian Paul Hardy was invited by the Glenbow Museum to put together a show based on their vast collection of artifacts. The result, *Kaleidoscopic Animalia*, was a series of fantasy window displays that explored the rich (and occasionally disturbing) history of our use of animals as both material and inspiration for fashion and design. Like Angela Waldie, Calgary artist Lisa Brawn finds inspiration in the humble chickadee. She has been carefully observing the birds of Calgary for years, using them as inspiration for her art. We include an interview and a series of woodcuts from Brawn, whose strikingly graphic images of wild birds have been seen around the world. In the final essay, I discuss Yvonne Mullock's installation and video *Dark Horse*, which was being presented by Stride Gallery during Stampede Week. Mullock's work, which uses a horse-powered press to make prints by crushing cowboy hats, responds in interesting ways to the issues raised by Susan Nance's more historical account of the horse named Greasy Sal. Whereas some of the other artists find inspiration in animals, Mullock often includes animals in the art-making process, challenging our ideas of who or what can produce art, and even what art is.

As this last example shows, although we have separated the essays into distinct groups, there is a dense web of parallels and exchanges between them. Seeing the similarities and the differences in the way that scholars, artists, and animal welfare advocates think about our relation to non-human animals opens up these conversation in multiple, productive ways. While Sean Kheraj charts the disappearance of domestic livestock from the city, it is notable that the City of Calgary's Biodiversity Strategy proposes the experimental use of goats to control weeds in city parks. (At the Community Seminar, one group suggested using community-owned goats that could be sold for meat at the end of the summer, an idea that was met with some resistance.) Lisa Brawn portrays the same birds that Gus Yaki sights along the Bow River, although she documents their presence in different ways, for different reasons. Shelley M. Alexander raises issues that prompt us to rethink our interactions with animals in the city; the people at the Calgary Wildlife Rehabilitation Centre deal with the consequences of these failed interactions every day. On a lighter note, while Kimberley Cooper talks about imitating insects, Mohammad Sadeghi Esfahlani talks about eating them. What all of the essays have in common is a desire to understand better the role that animals play in our urban life, and in our imaginations. If they collectively demonstrate the truth of the anthropologist Claude Lévi-Strauss's observation that "animals are good to think [with],"[2] they share in the belief that animals are good to live with as well.

sean kheraj

york university

how canadians used to live with livestock in cities

Calgary's city council has twice rejected proposals to permit residents to raise chickens in the city. In 2010 and 2015, a majority of council members voted against proposals for limited pilot programs for urban chicken raising. City councillors continue to refuse to accept the idea of urban livestock husbandry for Calgary.[3]

Paul Hughes, a Calgary resident, leads an organization called Canadian Liberated Urban Chicken Klub (CLUCK) that has fought for the legalization of urban chicken raising in Canada for several years. This food justice group advocates for the expansion of urban agriculture and livestock husbandry as a way of forging closer connections between urban dwellers and the food they eat. His group has now twice unsuccessfully sought to establish pilot urban chicken programs in Calgary.[4]

In the most recent debate over backyard chickens, councillors expressed concerns over a number of key issues associated with raising chickens in a city. Their concerns included noises, smells, the threat of disease, the management of unwanted and stray animals, and the cost of enforcing regulations. In spite of the support of the mayor and five members of council, the motion to approve a small pilot program for twenty households to begin raising chickens in the inner city failed to convince the nine opposing councillors. The City of Calgary's Responsible Pet Ownership Bylaw continues, therefore, to prohibit livestock husbandry in the city. According to the city's animal services policy:

> Farm animals kept in residential backyards or commercial spaces are generally inappropriate for a dense urban environment. Keeping such animals introduces problems into the neighbourhood such as noise, odors and pests attracted to the animal's food and hay. And an urban environment doesn't provide an ideal living space for farm animals.[5]

In Calgary, there is no place for livestock husbandry in the city.

Calgary is not alone in its resistance to urban livestock. In recent years, Toronto has also rejected proposals to introduce backyard chicken programs. One councillor in Toronto flatly objected to the idea that livestock have any appropriate place in an urban environment. During one debate Councillor Frances Nunziata said, "If you want to have chickens then buy a farm, go to a farm."[6] From this perspective, livestock husbandry should be an exclusively rural practice.

Woman carrying a live hen on Kensington Avenue, Toronto ca. 1926.
Source: City of Toronto Archives, Fonds 1266, Item 8245.

While city councils in Calgary and Toronto have refused to reform their bylaws to accommodate chickens in their urban environments, other cities in Canada have begun to embrace the notion of urban livestock. In British Columbia, city councils in Victoria, Vancouver, Surrey, and Kelowna have all approved limited backyard chicken programs in recent years, encouraging residents to raise small numbers of hens to produce eggs. Montreal and Gatineau have approved similar programs in Quebec. While the specifics of each program varies, the intent is to allow urban dwellers to raise these small livestock animals in cities as a form of urban agriculture.

In Alberta, the City of Edmonton has already approved a pilot program for backyard chicken raising. In 2014, the city council voted in favour of implementing what it called an "Urban Hen Keeping Pilot Project" in partnership with River City Chickens Collective, a local urban agriculture advocacy group. The city selected nineteen sites where homeowners raised small numbers of hens under relatively strict animal control regulations. The pilot households had to register their animals with the province for identification and tracking. They also had to seek consent from their neighbours.[7]

Throughout the first year of the project, the nineteen sites were subject to inspection by the city to ensure that the participants adhered to the guidelines and regulations. After a year, the Urban Hen Keeping Pilot Project submitted a summary report to the Community Services Committee outlining the success of its first phase. Over the course of one year, eighteen of the nineteen pilot sites were found to be compliant with city regulations or eventually became compliant by the end of the year (one household withdrew from the program over concerns about the mandatory run enclosure for the hens). Six of the pilot sites received a total of twelve animal control complaints. Animal control peace officers investigated all complaints and found that five complaints were in reference to nuisance birds feeding on food and waste, four focused on hens running at large off premises, two complaints were found concerning foul smells, and one complaint about noise. The pilot project's first year resulted in no concerns or complaints over coyotes or other predatory wildlife, and the report also failed to find any link between the size of a property or proximity to a neighbour as a cause of complaints. The Community Services Committee agreed to renew the project and approve its second phase with the expansion of test sites throughout the city.[8]

Of course, the raising of chickens and other livestock animals in Canadian cities is not a novel concept. Domestic livestock animals were once vital and common actors in urban life in Canada.[9] In the nineteenth and early twentieth centuries, livestock husbandry was an ordinary part of life in cities. Most critically, livestock animals provided food and labour. The streetscapes of Toronto, Montreal, Winnipeg, Vancouver, and, yes, even Calgary once included cattle, pigs, chickens, and horses. Livestock weren't just "farm animals."

As municipal governments across the country continue to debate whether or not to permit chicken raising, they confront a regulatory challenge that was once commonplace and a central function of urban governance in the nineteenth century. Managing a growing urban environment that could accommodate livestock animals was one of the primary roles of municipal governments. In the nineteenth century, cities across Canada developed bylaws to regulate the use of livestock animals for a number of purposes. They passed bylaws to regulate the raising of animals for food and labour. They regulated the use of horses as a mode of transportation. They established and regulated public markets where live animals were sold and slaughtered. They also regulated butchers and slaughterhouses. They inspected milk quality at urban dairies. When livestock animals died, cities had to determine the procedures for the removal and disposal of animal carcasses. Municipal governments even had rules for how to remove the piles of manure that accumulated on the streets. In general, municipalities in the nineteenth century sought to establish rules and regulations that would allow for the efficient exploitation of livestock animals because those animals were necessary for the growth and development of cities.

When developing bylaws to govern livestock husbandry in cities, municipal governments in Canada tended to focus on two primary concerns: property relations and public health. These are some of the same concerns facing city councils today in the debate over backyard chickens. Through a series of different bylaws, municipal governments juggled the competing interests of a number of different parties, including landowners, the owners of livestock, pedestrians, streetcar companies, the general public health, and the animals themselves.

The first livestock regulatory challenge cities faced was the problem of animal trespass. In the nineteenth century, it was common for Canadians to raise livestock without enclosures, a practice known as free-range livestock husbandry. A cow or a pig could be left to roam and forage unattended. This saved the owner the time and expense of having to lead his or her animals to pasture or to supply the animals with expensive fodder. Pigs were especially talented independent foragers that found plenty to eat on the streets of Canada's growing cities. Most early bylaws in cities such as Montreal and Toronto featured restrictions on free-roaming pigs. Montreal had prohibited free-running pigs as early as 1810.[10] Toronto similarly banned the unrestricted movement of pigs in the city in its earliest nuisance bylaw in 1834 but still ran into difficulty controlling the wily creatures. Throughout the 1830s, the city council in Toronto received numerous petitions signed by dozens of residents complaining of the problem of free-roaming pigs and cattle in the city.[11] These complaints compelled city governments to hire pound-keepers and establish city pounds for the capture of stray animals. In Montreal, the city empowered all police to impound stray livestock. In 1892, for instance, the Montreal police impounded more than 800 animals, including horses, sheep, cows, and pigs.[12]

Free-roaming animals caused a number of difficulties for Canada's industrial cities of the nineteenth century. They obstructed street traffic and blocked passage for residents on increasingly crowded sidewalks. In 1874, the *Daily Free Press* in Winnipeg complained of the streets being infested with pigs and other animals that made it difficult for residents to get around the city. It even noted the obstructions that stubborn pigs could cause by digging and burying themselves in the drains along the side of roads.[13]

More difficult, however, were the property conflicts livestock animals triggered with their free-roaming behaviour. Hungry cattle and pigs paid no mind to the private property boundaries of urban residents. They broke fences, wandered into gardens to feed on whatever they could find, and left their waste behind nearly everywhere they journeyed. In 1872, the *Toronto Mail* noted the continued difficulty residents faced in protecting their floral beds and grass plots from "the cravings of the never-to-be-satisfied porcine stomach."[14] In 1879, Richard Code, a property owner in Winnipeg, captured several horses and cattle that had destroyed the fence surrounding his market garden and eaten his produce. He petitioned the city council for compensation for the damage to his property. Livestock owners, however, could also lay claim to damage to their animals as a form of property. In the same year that Richard Code sought recompense for the damage to his market garden. Andrew Boyd, a milk dealer in Winnipeg, also sought compensation for the death of one of his cows that died as a result of eating garbage at the municipal nuisance ground where the city had failed to construct a fence around the growing pile of refuse.[15] Four petitioners in Toronto in 1883 successfully won cash payments from the city to make up for the loss of sheep to stray dogs.[16] The regulation of livestock in nineteenth-century urban environments balanced the property interests of landowners and livestock owners.

In addition to protecting property interests, municipal governments in nineteenth-century Canadian cities also sought to mitigate the potential harmful public health effects

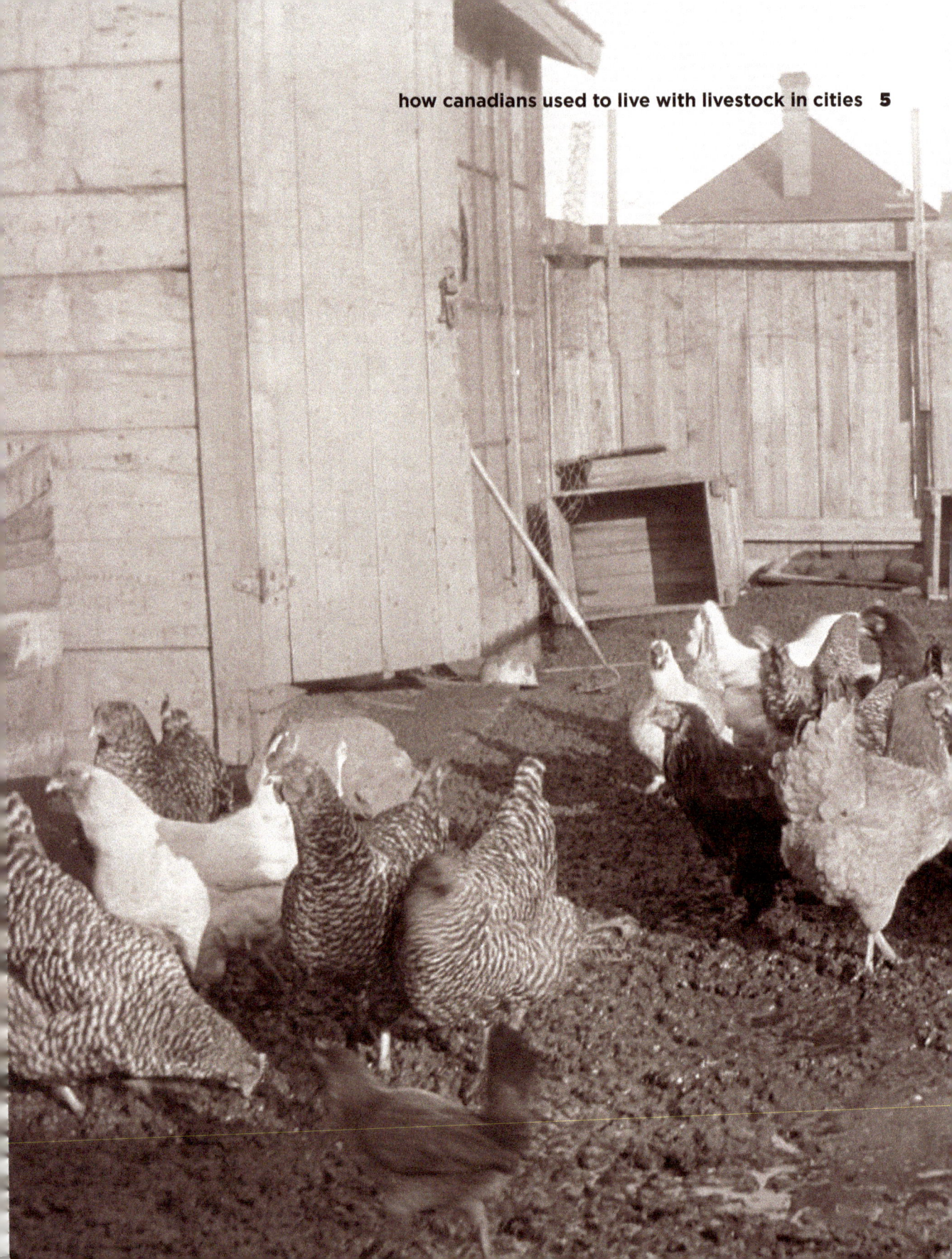

of urban livestock husbandry. During a time when Canadians believed that foul-smelling airs could cause illness, animal waste and carcasses drew specific concern. Nineteenth-century public health bylaws in Canadian cities, therefore, often focused much attention on animal bodies and waste in an effort to protect public health. Early nuisance and public health bylaws in Montreal, Toronto, Winnipeg, and Vancouver all attempted to address the problem of rotting animal carcasses that could be found in city streets. Daily city newspapers regularly kept track of the problem of animal carcasses. "A dead horse lies off Mill street in the common," noted the *Montreal Daily Witness* in September 1874.[17] To combat this problem, cities across Canada passed nuisance and public health bylaws requiring livestock owners to properly dispose of their dead animals. They also established municipal dumps and pits where residents could deposit dead animals, and prohibited the dumping of animal bodies in adjacent rivers and lakes. This was especially troublesome in Toronto and Winnipeg, where the Don and Red Rivers respectively could be found teeming with piles of dead horses, cattle, and pigs. In Winnipeg, the problem of animal carcasses was so severe in the 1880s that the city's public health officer complained that residents were failing to bury their dead animals, as required by the city's public health bylaw. Instead, they were dragging the bodies just beyond the city limits and abandoning them in a large pile that accumulated to more than 180 carcasses by 1883.[18] In Montreal, city police were responsible for disposing of abandoned animal carcasses. They handled hundreds of carcasses every year. For example, in 1887, the police found a record 119 dead horses in city streets.[19]

Toward the end of the nineteenth century, municipal governments started to use public health bylaws to significantly restrict urban livestock husbandry. Sanitary reformers and some urban residents began to raise concerns about the potential adverse health effects of keeping animals in the city. They also expressed aesthetic objections to the presence of livestock. This often reflected particular class and ethnic perceptions of the urban environment that worked against the economic interests of the working-class populations of Canadian cities. In Montreal, sanitary reformers and public health officials targeted pigs as a health risk to urban residents. In doing so, they directed their complaints at working-class French Canadian and Irish residents of the city who kept livestock to supplement family incomes and make ends meet. In 1865, the *Montreal Herald* complained about piggeries in Griffintown, an Irish immigrant and working-class district, where it claimed that the pigs were kept "in a most filthy condition, and highly injurious to health as well as offensive to the eye."[20] By 1874, Montreal outlawed the keeping of pigs in all parts of the city and by 1876 no person was permitted to keep a livestock animal within a house or tenement.

In Toronto, public health officials and sanitary reformers raised concerns over cattle byres or stables. Urban dairies were once a common amenity in Canadian cities, supplying fresh milk on a daily basis. By the 1870s, larger dairies and swill milk operations in Toronto drew negative public attention from nearby residents who complained of horrific smells and waste. The swill milk facilities of Gooderham and Worts at the mouth of the Don River and smaller cattle byres in other parts of the central city eventually led residents to pressure the council to ban cattle from the city.[21] In 1882, the city amended the nuisance bylaw to restrict the number of cattle that could be kept on an individual property, pushing all dairies to the fringes of the urban environment in Toronto.

By the late nineteenth century, Vancouver residents had taken aim at slaughterhouses. Beginning in 1887, the city council regulated the placement of slaughterhouses in the city with the intent of preventing such facilities from becoming a threat to the public health.[22] Property owners living near some of the city's earliest slaughterhouses, however, continuously complained to the city council of smells and other nuisances they believed threatened their health. For instance, in 1889, residents south of False Creek sent multiple petitions to the city council calling for the removal of nearby slaughterhouses. Within a year, the city passed a new bylaw prohibiting slaughterhouses from establishing within the city limits. The city closed a number of slaughterhouses and destroyed their animals in the process of moving slaughtering of live animals outside the city limits.[23]

By the end of the nineteenth century, the examples of pigs in Montreal, cattle in Toronto, and slaughterhouses in Vancouver revealed an increasing discomfort among some Canadian urban dwellers with the presence of livestock in cities. To be sure, that discomfort was based on a combination of public health fears, class and ethnic bias, and aesthetic perceptions of the urban environment. By the early decades of the twentieth century, Canadians kept fewer large livestock animals in cities but continued to raise large numbers of small animals, such as chickens. In 1891, the census recorded 13,706 chickens in Vancouver, nearly one for each of the 13,709 people who lived in the city.[24] Large livestock animal owners certainly may have faced pressure from changing public health bylaws to remove their animals from the city, but they also faced practical pressures to abandon urban livestock husbandry as cities became more densely settled with people living in smaller spaces. Technological changes also contributed to the decline of urban livestock in cities. The electrification of street railways and the popularization of the automobile made the horse obsolete. Refrigeration technologies, railways, and the industrialization of dairying and meat packing contributed to the geographic displacement of cattle from cities as urban residents in Canada were drawn to the conven-

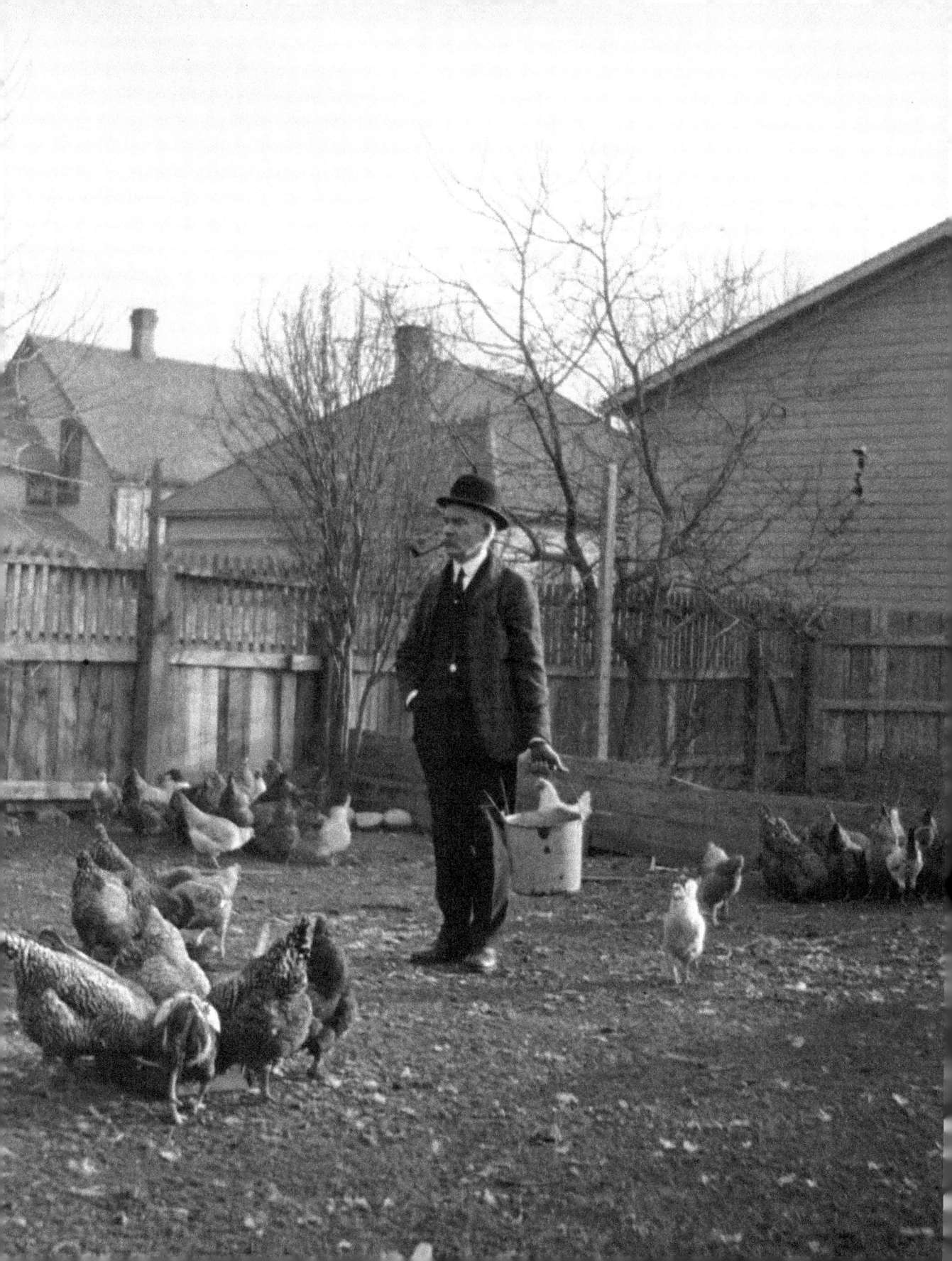

ience of purchasing milk and meat that was delivered to urban markets from adjacent rural areas. Canadians were not simply forced to stop raising animals in cities by changing bylaws. They also opted for the conveniences that further dissociated urban life from the visceral and sensory experiences of livestock husbandry.

What, then, can Canadians learn from the experiences of urban residents and livestock in the past? First, many of the regulatory challenges that cities faced concerning livestock are the same as those confronted by cities that have adopted backyard chicken programs today. The first report on the pilot project in Edmonton cited a number of concerns that nineteenth-century cities also faced: free-roaming animals, smells, waste, and public health concerns. Nineteenth-century urban livestock husbandry operated under municipal regulation to mitigate against property conflicts and adverse public health effects. Efforts to re-introduce urban livestock husbandry will likely also involve the establishment of a regulatory regime to accommodate chickens and other livestock animals.

Second, nineteenth-century urban livestock regulations did not take into consideration the interactions of livestock and wild animals. As the Edmonton pilot program found, there were no problems yet with predatory species. However, wild birds eating stray feed became a nuisance in the first year of the program. The growing population of wild urban animals, including raccoons, coyotes, and rats, raises new concerns over the effects of introducing livestock animals to urban environments in Canada.

Finally, livestock husbandry in the nineteenth century was, in many instances, a necessity of urban life. Raising a pig or a cow or a chicken helped to feed families. Keeping a horse was often critical for transportation or the operation of a business. The slaughtering of live animals at public markets, butcher shops, and abattoirs was once the only option for accessing fresh meats in a city. Technological changes rendered many of these practices obsolete because they were less convenient and more expensive. Livestock husbandry in cities today will not likely fulfill the same economic role that it once did in the nineteenth century. It will play new economic and even socio-cultural roles, and regulations will have to reflect that. Harvesting an egg from a chicken raised in your backyard may be costlier than simply purchasing an egg from a supermarket, but the experience of developing direct connections between food production and consumption in cities may have positive effects on how we think about our broader relationship to the urban environments in which we live.

James C. Linton feeding chickens in yard of Linton family home, Calgary, Alberta. 1913, Glenbow Archives, NA-5610-30, Calgary, AB.

outlaw horses & the

Unnamed grey horse, possibly Greasy Sal, performing as outlaw.
Souvenir postcard, 1928. Glenbow Archives, NA-2365-10, Calgary, AB.

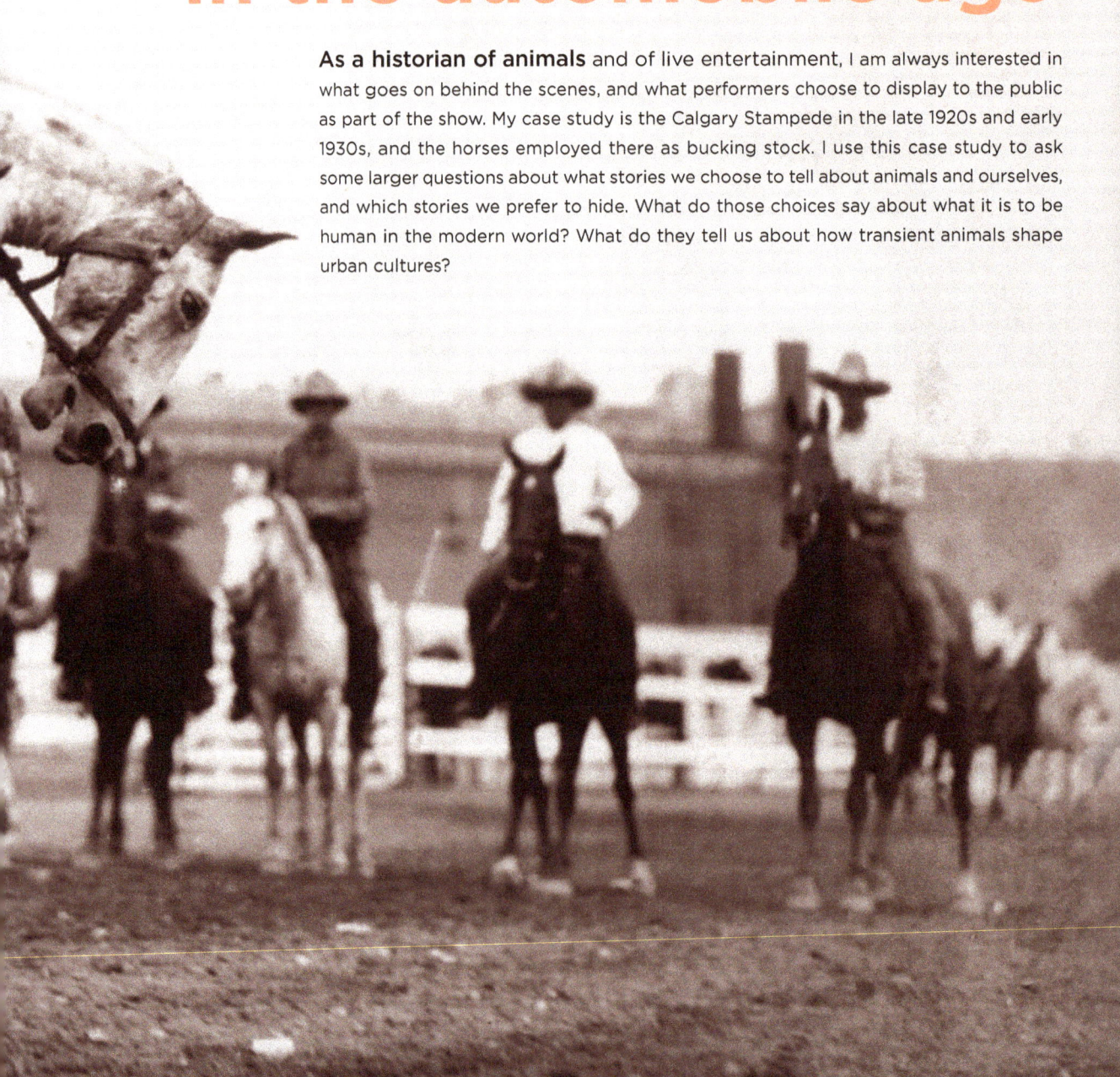

susan nance
university of guelph

true spirit of calgary
in the automobile age

As a historian of animals and of live entertainment, I am always interested in what goes on behind the scenes, and what performers choose to display to the public as part of the show. My case study is the Calgary Stampede in the late 1920s and early 1930s, and the horses employed there as bucking stock. I use this case study to ask some larger questions about what stories we choose to tell about animals and ourselves, and which stories we prefer to hide. What do those choices say about what it is to be human in the modern world? What do they tell us about how transient animals shape urban cultures?

In my research on animals, performance, and modernity in early twentieth-century cities I am especially interested in how Calgarians and others constructed a city marketing brand—the "spirit of Calgary," as they would have said at the time—and how they imagined it could help the city invite investment and trade. Connected to this question of what Calgarian civic branding looked like is the issue of what modernity meant for horses and people in "the West."

Founded in 1912, the Calgary Stampede is one of Canada's oldest and most controversial public celebrations—"Cowtown's sacred cow"—and constitutes a brand for the city of Calgary while serving internationally as a premier event in professional rodeo.[25] Juxtaposing old practices of ranch-based production and new modes of sports consumption in a highly stylized way, by the 1920s already these performances represented the globalized beef industry's contribution to the world of entertainment, which rodeo people shaped in reference to the global economy's Western-themed entertainments.

In Calgary, and beyond, people used rodeo competitions to define their communities by their particular relationships to perceived-Western animals and the landscapes they inhabited. Although today people think of the white cowboy hat as a sign of Stampede hospitality, the dynamic image of a bucking bronc with rider was an early icon of the Calgary Stampede, and the ostensible city spirit. Westerners claimed authority over those animals and spaces through competitive riding or roping of unbroken cattle and horses. Many urban Calgarians seemed to see the Stampede as an opportunity for self-exoticization by monopolizing particular for-profit performance opportunities only Westerners could claim. Here was a case of city people appropriating rural culture to their own advantage.

I am interested not only in the rodeo animal celebrities (Steamboat, Midnight, Tornado, Red Rock, or Bodacious) but the common rodeo animals whose experiences were more typical. So, I've gone in search of a long-forgotten grey mare whom people called Greasy Sal.

Her life was reflective of those of the hundreds of other horses who played a particular kind of "Western" horse in rodeo shows, namely the bronc outlaw. This equine character was produced at the intersection of wild horse behaviour, local business cultures, and the Western genre and seems to have appealed specifically to rodeo people and audiences living on the cusp of the post-equine era in North America (1910–1930), in which most people no longer employed horses for labour. That is, Greasy Sal as bronc outlaw was a post-equine horse employed primarily for nostalgic entertainment purposes—just (and this is important, I think) as people were transitioning to the gasoline engine.

Early rodeos reflected the pragmatic (paradoxical?) agricultural values of their participants—wherein horses were at times beloved individuals, at times a perishable commodity, and the environment both helper and enemy of man—blended with the marketing goals of the local rodeo committee, newspapers, tourist magazines, the railways, hotel owners, and other parties looking to boost the local economy. This diverse group was loosely united around the goal of transforming decidedly unglamorous animal management work (like calf roping and horse breaking) and drunken ranch pastimes called "cowboy sports" (like bull riding) into news and entertainment that would somehow convey a personality for the city.

Looking back across a century, the real spirit of Calgary can still be difficult to pin down, as though to Calgarians the concept was so obvious no one needed to define it. Various amiable city editorials and histories have offered, for instance, "confidence [and] community spirit" (1923) or "brashness, optimism, and resilience" (1994) as definitions.[26] Why did prominent Calgarians imagine a rodeo competition loosely based on rural ranch life would effectively communicate this self-mythologizing concept?

Calgarians who endorsed the rodeo (and there was initially considerable debate about why a Wild West–style competition was appropriate for the city) would labour diligently to define themselves comprehensibly as Westerners and brand themselves with an attitude toward life that relished challenging labour, persevered in contexts in which others failed, and valued personal independence and self-sufficiency. The Stampede's competitive events would perform these usually unspoken values, only vaguely encapsulated as the "cowboy spirit." Rodeo events challenged humans against cattle and horses, whom viewers were encouraged to interpret as "Western" because they resisted human control. And, somehow, the collective fiction portrayed by competitive performances of human versus quasi-feral / "half-wild" animals came to symbolize the city's modern business brand, perhaps because they performed a metaphorical moment symbolizing infinite possibility.

Consider also the broader anthrozoological context. Across the continent, an urbanizing public was increasingly alienated from holistic experiences of the livestock upon which they relied materially. Urbanites had the luxury of growing squeamish and sentimental about animals while still demanding steak on the plate as a key indicator of middle-class

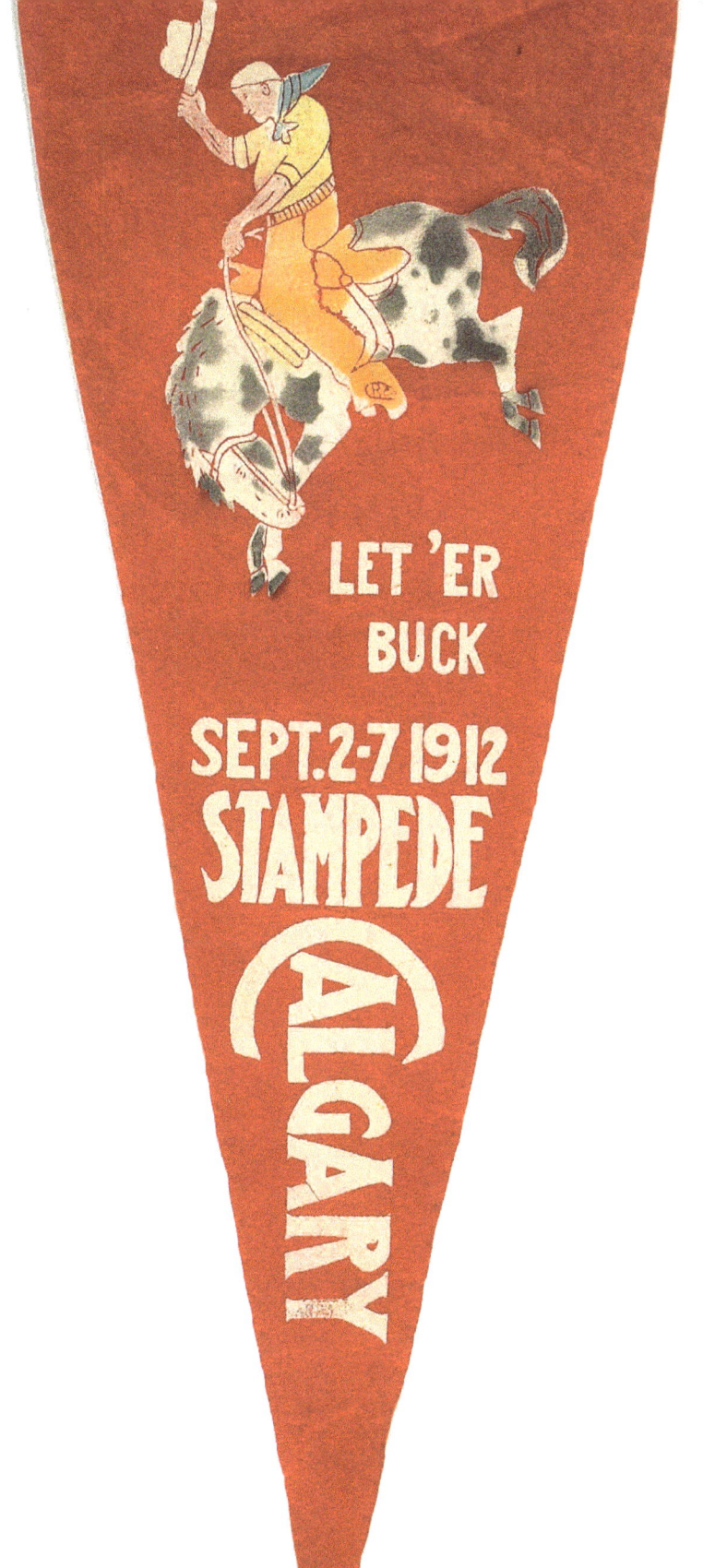

LET 'ER BUCK

SEPT. 2-7 1912

STAMPEDE

CALGARY

status. Accordingly, rodeo people found themselves in a difficult position. They sought to define their region with representations of the labour that produced beef and gentle dude ranch horses before an audience of visitors unused to and potentially shocked by such things. At the same time, the urban Calgarians and rural Albertans who brought the event to life were themselves also consumers who experienced the contradiction of sentimentality and consumption. There were no dyads here but a number of overlapping moral economies as rodeo people worked out how to talk about horses and cattle to themselves and outsiders.

Early audiences also intervened, and that first decade, ticket sales, arena talk, and press reviews made it clear that spectators wanted to see rodeo sports that were difficult and violent, but not deadly. The balance of rodeo events (if we exclude team roping, pageants, parades, and contract acts) demonstrated "raw challenge and excitement,"[27] and dramatic, explosive action, not finesse. Wild horses drawn from rangelands in Alberta, Montana, and Wyoming bore the burden of living up to the ideals of bronc-ness that rodeo committees had invented. Regarding competitors from Montana who might invest in a trip to Stampede, for instance, Guy Weadick promised the secretary of the Montana State Fair in Helena: "For the bucking contest here, . . . I would say to you, that we are going to have [the] buckinest bucking horses that ever bucked a buck."[28] Talk in the business often fetishized the "buck" as evidence of horses who, rodeo people argued, enjoyed struggling against a rider, who were mean cusses and born fighters, "real bad ones," as the lore held.[29]

From the beginning, the bucker—the "outlaw" bronc—dominated the show and its iconography, effectively demonstrating to viewers and participants how a "Western" animal behaved and reflected upon the character of Western people. Bronc riding, with its bounding, kicking horses, "wrecks," and cowboy injuries, epitomized early rodeo as (what today we would call) an adrenalin sport. The practice also fostered breathless press and magazine publicity.

Hence, Greasy Sal, a grey mare from rural Alberta. She was a work-a-day Stampede bronc whose barely recorded life history exposes the backstage reality that facilitated the front region performances of outlaw bucker. The Stampede employed her in the Canadian saddle bronc competition for several years in the late 1920s, then briefly as a bareback riding horse until she disappeared from the historical record around 1931. Greasy Sal was among the twenty or so broncs owned for a time by the Calgary Industrial Exhibition Company. Out at the Stampede Ranch, as it would become known, staff managed a cache of horses, sometimes lending them out to other rodeos. They also rented horses from private individuals, sometimes a competitor who might have a couple of "bad ones" he brought to Stampede to defer costs, and a number of whom made a serious business of finding proven buckers and contracting them out. Although the cowboy persona may have served as the human face of the rodeo sports, the stock contractor was already an equally important producer behind "the show." Local ranchers and rural people supplied the bulk of the Stampede's horses, and plenty wrote letters to Guy Weadick offering and advocating for their stock to supplement income earned competing or working around the grounds for $10 per day.

Greasy Sal had thusly been purchased in 1926 from a contractor named Jim McNab of Macleod (now Fort Macleod) Alberta, through the Stampede's stockman, Clem Gardiner.[30] Typically, Greasy Sal performed for two or three of the seven days of the show along with many dozens of others, all indicated with a brand and a show name in the Stampede's horse lists. She and the other rough stock horses were valued from $100 to $200 each.[31] In 1927 Greasy Sal was one of 195 broncs employed at the Stampede,[32] and one of the 267 bucked in 1929.[33] These totals give an indication how resource intensive Stampede managers found it to produce the kind of bucking performances riders and audiences demanded; the process demanded a sort of mass production of bucking.

In those days, rodeos also began limiting rough stock rides to a maximum of eight seconds, with chutes and grandstands arranged to provide spectators with the best view of the action. Judges awarded animal and rider points for the quality of the performance determined by particular criteria. This innovation saved equine energy while reducing the possibility of an animal losing the will to buck by inadvertently being broken while at the rodeo. As such, these equine performers became modern post-equine horses. One did not do more than get them halter-broken. One did not plow a field with or ride to church on such horses, nor drive such horses on hoof to the show. One hauled them in a pickup truck trailer or in a rail car. All their labour and value was focused on their behaviour in the arena.

To the horses scouted and reserved for rodeo use, the process of bucking was one in which they successfully freed themselves of a rider every time and learned just how to do so as quickly as possible. The modern bucking process essentially displayed the effects of operant conditioning on a horse, which rodeo people colloquially described as an innate "love" of bucking off a rider. In fact, the raw ingredients for the outlaw bronc were simply a horse who tended toward fighting and kicking (rather than running), unaccustomed to riders, flanked in a chute, and rewarded for his or her bucking behaviour after eight seconds. Stampede officials and chute managers instituted these and other innovations to appease local critics who argued that the Stampede should present an ideal of Western life free of unacceptable animal suffering or egregious displays of obvious cruelty. So, after 1919, the Stampede excluded various traditional events that led reticent or inactive animals to bleed, pass out, break legs, or lose body parts (horns) before an audience (although all of these things happened occasionally anyway).[34]

Living horses like Greasy Sal unknowingly played the outlaw bronc in a broader graphic and storytelling context in which "Western" stories featured shootouts, chases, and other dramatic action. The horses who could produce the fetishized "buck" (many failed to perform consistently and were weeded out of the bucking strings supplied to the Stampede) contributed to the rodeo-wide convention for presentation of horses as outlaw buckers in flight—not grazing on a remote hillside, or waiting in a paddock behind the arena, or being petted by a pretty girl dressed in fancy Western attire, but rather at their most explosively violent.

Why so? Rodeo committees had discovered early on that this icon and the corresponding horse behaviour sold tickets. The iconography of the outlaw bronc and cowboy offered a recognizable truth about Western horses and people, and so it was reproduced. In time, the bronc became the most dependable, consumer-friendly icon of the accepted/proposed truths about Calgary as a Western city, uniquely tied to nature yet ready for business. And Calgarians employed this horsey character to claim authority over this unexpected symbol of Western modernity to the extent that the horse who did not jump and buck in expected ways appeared to rodeo judges, riders, and audiences as substandard, and deserving of a low score or generating a re-ride for the cowboy or cowgirl in question.

Horse naming practices enhanced this tradition and added entertainment value to broncs by emphasizing the "buck," the cowboy's experience of the ride, and the acrobatics of preferred horses: Elevator, Jim Stink, Corkskrew, Zig Zag, Earthquake, Cyclone, Explosion, Flying Devil, Night Mare, Funeral Wagon, Calamity Ann.[35] Greasy Sal herself took a name that indicated riders would have a difficult time staying on her back. Other names integrated rodeo with broader continental cultural economies by endorsing audience knowledge of contemporary popular culture and trends, cinema, celebrities, or Wild West clichés: Alberta Kid, Sox (baseball), The Sheik (in 1927 in reference to the famous Valentino films), King Tut (whose relics had recently been discovered in Egypt),

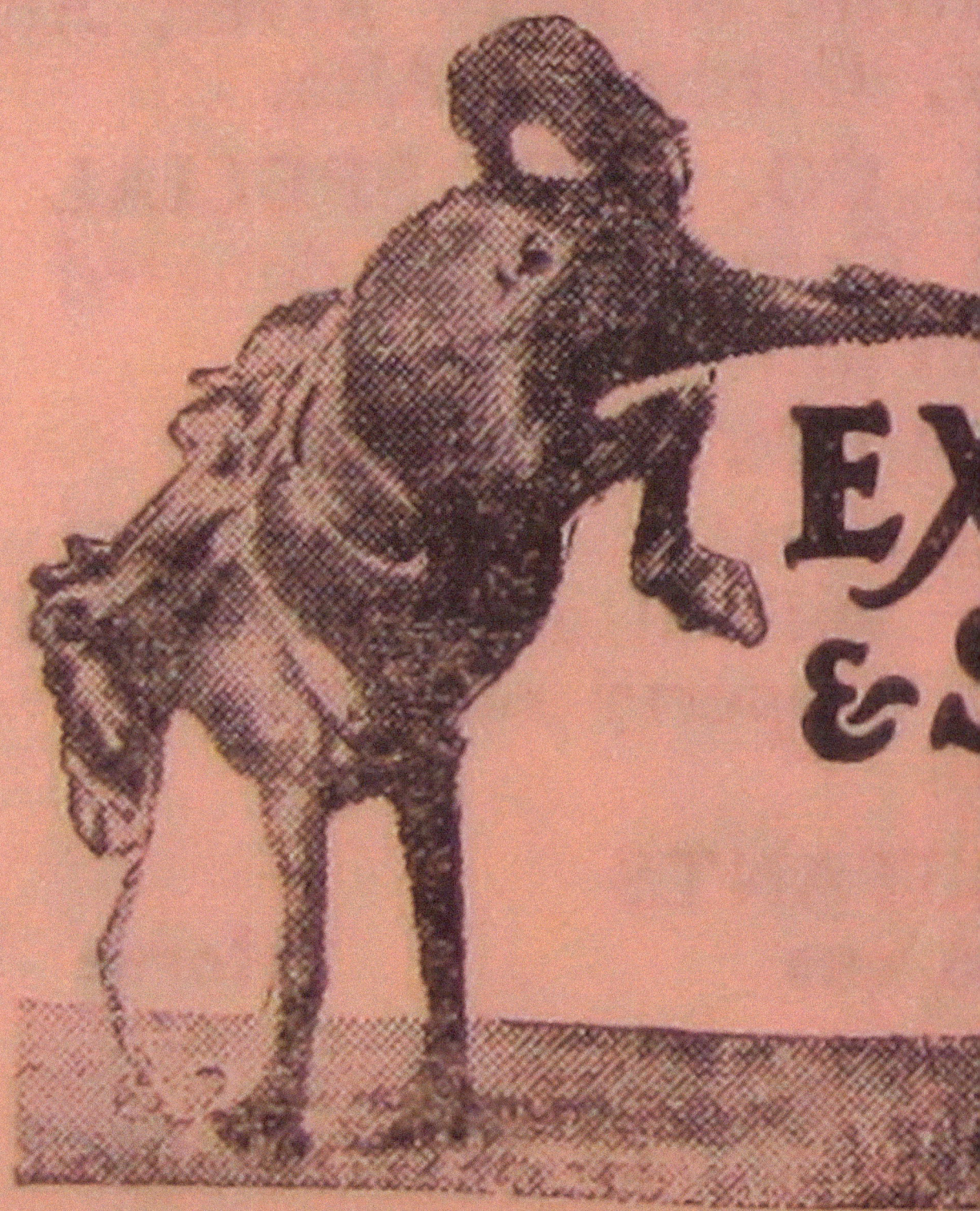

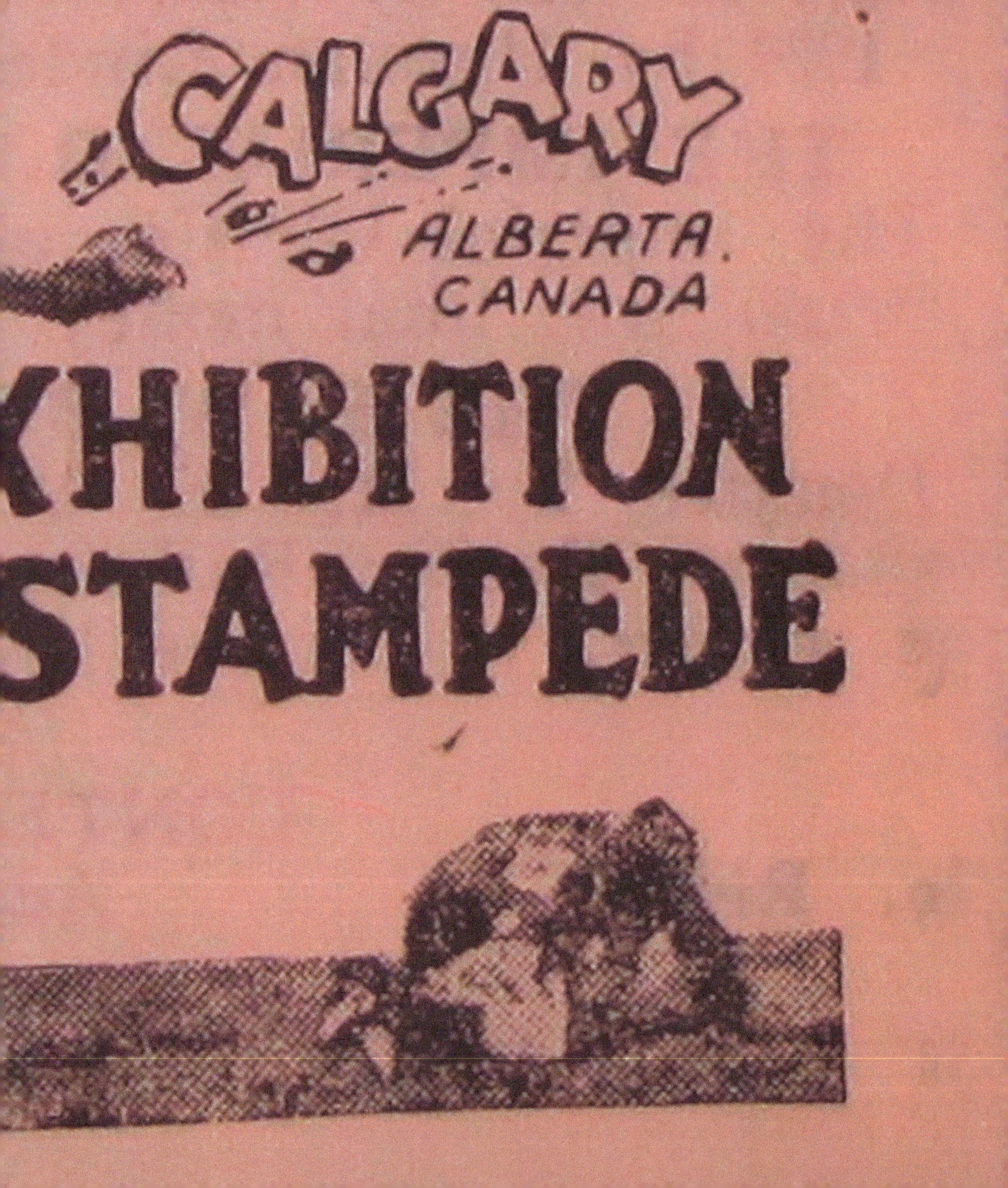

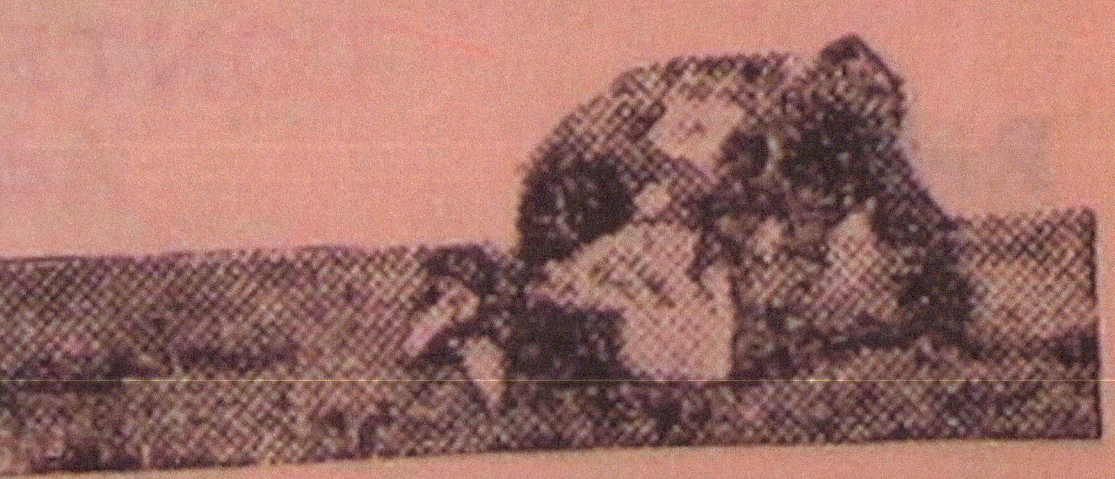

Lindbergh (1927), and Dirty Dora (to lampoon the "Dumb Dora" comic strip). Horses marketed as such to rodeo audiences were consumer-oriented creatures, defined solely by their few minutes in the chute, and the ten or twenty seconds in the arena.

This was front stage information.

Indeed, audiences knew Greasy Sal only when she performed at Stampede each year between 1927 and 1930, as the arena announcer called out her name to the crowds each time she was ridden. Stampede records from 1927 also show that she was lent, leased, or sent to another (unnamed) rodeo in the care of Clem Gardiner, at which time Gardiner marked her on the back of his horse delivery list as out of the running there: "X in foal."[36]

This was decidedly backstage information.

In 1930, Greasy Sal foaled again at the Stampede Ranch. What happened to the first of these young horses is not apparent in Stampede records. But of the 1930 birth, in late May that year Dick Cosgrove reported to Guy Weadick: "Gray Mare branded D2 I think she is called Grizley Sal [sic] she had a colt two weeks ago and I killed it."[37] Two other proven buckers, Baby Doll and Red Head, were also about to give birth but nonetheless bucked again at Stampede later that year, with no foals in tow bawling for their mothers and distracting these mares from the arena performance. In fact, Cosgrove had promised Weadick that the three would "be dry and in shape in time for the show."[38]

From a rodeo point of view, Greasy Sal and other mares were modern performers with a message to deliver, more valuable bucking than caring for a baby. Greasy Sal as mare (rather than outlaw bronc as she was presented to the public) would have grieved the loss of her foal, spent a period of days or weeks calling and pacing the pasture looking for him or her. That aspect of her existence is an element we must consider in order to have a more holistic understanding of her as a historical being with concerns beyond the bucking chute. That aspect of her life exposes the degree to which Westerners constructed themselves by shaping very particular public understandings of animals. Did Dick Cosgrove think about how his act of dispatching a newborn horse, which many consumers would have taken as symbolic of innocence, beauty, and optimism for the future, defied the claims Stampede participants made to have unique insight into and the authority over the West?

By 1930, Greasy Sal was nearing the end of her tenure at Stampede. She was noted on one horse list in a group marked "These horses not very good," soon to be weeded out of the bucking string.[39] Other horses—Alberta Kid, Sliptivity, Santa Claus, Honorable Patches, Tennessee, Big Smoke, Dirty Dora—seemed to still be bucking from Greasy Sal's original 1926 cohort (while the rest were all of more recent vintage).[40] It appears that for most horses the average number of years at Stampede was perhaps three to five, which was about the average length of time cart horses spent hauling in cities when they were employed by the millions in the equine era.[41] In some ways, the Stampede's outlaw broncs were not so different from their turn-of-the-century urban workhorse kin, except that they were transients who passed through the city leaving only their images and hoof prints behind.

The Stampede's meaning was infused with an ideology that rejected public talk of animal suffering in order to support the myth that broncs like Greasy Sal (or her foal?) were certainly not disposable but in fact enthusiastic participants in the adventure that was the interwar West.

Many rodeo people probably just took it for granted that to talk about events such as the killing of Greasy Sal's foal was inappropriate. In modern Calgary, many people might have found themselves in a "confused state of mind" as they struggled to reconcile protective desires toward animals with humankind's accelerating and clearly self-enriching manipulation and consumption of them. Modern animals like the outlaw bronc who hankers for a fight and "just loves to buck" were creatures Calgarians and their visitors—many of them increasingly alienated from holistic knowledge of work animals—employed to paper over this paradox while (somehow!) also branding the city with a can-do spirit that said: "We're open for business!"[42]

Greasy Sal's job was to represent the hope that cowboys and Westerners had a unique hardiness and optimism, and could balance the contradictions inherent in modern life by being at once of nature and not of nature. People came to perceive bucking horses as representative of an authentically traditional "Western" cowboy spirit of individualism and perseverance (by representing the man's struggle against the forces of nature), although they were in fact signs of the ways industrialization and mass consumerism were changing Alberta forever.

silence of the song dogs

shelley m. alexander

university of calgary

Entertaining the notion of a City of Animals, we are challenged to accept animals like coyote: animals that are critical to biodiversity but confront our world order by sometimes living in our backyards, sometimes consuming our pets. We are required to envision how we can co-flourish, and to dream how we can fully consider these "others" –the non-human animals from which, Darwin so nicely articulated, we differ only by degree and not by kind. We must rethink our ideas of the human as central figure in this animal place. We must also visualize the expectations, ethics, and politics that entrain this place. As I see it, coyote marks our toughest journey of reconciling the self with "nature." Having circumvented the challenges of the human world, coyote has thrown down the gauntlet—in response, we must aspire to a higher consciousness and broader compassion. We must dream our song dog back home.

The challenge of embracing coyotes in the City of Animals begins with highly polarized beliefs about species: beliefs about where coyote belongs, which behaviours are appropriate around people, what rules govern the human-coyote relationship, and whether we should kill coyotes when they break with expected norms. The dichotomous beliefs surrounding this 35–40 lb. wild dog are echoed in the multitude of names given to it, including, among others: Song dog, Trickster, Creator, Killer, Invasive Species, and Pest. Distilled further, challenges arise because of a collective intolerance of innate coyote behaviours, particularly aggression toward pets and people (i.e., attacks). This, despite aggression being an evolved trait that confers survival to all dogs and a trait tolerated within bounds when perpetrated by the family dog. The lack of willingness to tolerate certain levels of aggression in coyotes results in routine execution of these animals in order to maintain safe cities or safe places for people. I dream of a City of Animals that is inclusive. But this will require shifting our collective boundaries and tolerances around species like coyotes (or raccoons, beavers, skunks, and other "typical pests"). This chapter explores some of the issues surrounding this long-standing and ever-changing relationship that may help us envision this new city—a city that embraces coyote.

coyote dreaming, acrylic on canvas, Shelley Alexander

human-coyote co-evolution

Our relationship with coyote encapsulates the dissonance in our negotiations with many animals, wild or urban. It raises tough ethical questions about the too-often ugly truths of our inhumanity toward all animals.

The human relationship with coyote is an enduring one, but it is only recently that it has become complicated, estranged, and sometimes unhappy. The archeological evidence shows coyote (*Canis latrans*) evolved and is only found on the North American continent. In its current form it has enjoyed ubiquitous distribution across the continent for over one million years. As species go, coyote is old. It has witnessed the rise and fall of such iconic species as the Woolly Mammoth, Dire Wolf, Sabre-Toothed Tiger, and countless others that migrated to this continent during the last great ice age. With human occupation estimated to be less than 15,000 years before present, one might argue that early humans actually co-evolved with coyotes on the Coyote Continent. Not surprisingly, because coyotes predate human occupation, the species holds a central and sometimes revered role in many Aboriginal stories. Coyote is trickster, song dog, shapeshifter, and creator: these evocative stories depict a deep, sometimes mystical relationship between early humans, coyotes, and the environment, while illuminating ecological facts about the species that have only recently been "discovered" by Western scientists.

Revered by North American Aboriginal cultures, coyotes were subsequently persecuted without restraint by European settlers from the mid-1800s onward. Coyotes were systematically killed en masse (along with other carnivores) as part of a continent-wide effort to sterilize the land and make it suitable for cultivation and stock production. The killing mentality has migrated across generations and space, to become, in some social sectors, a de facto way of living on the land—killing coyotes is just part of what you do. Today, there are few animal-related issues that polarize Canadians like coyotes. Media debate erupts at the mere mention of the species, yielding evidence of a growing sector that disapproves of killing coyotes. Despite that voice, coyotes still hold the unenviable title of North America's most persecuted carnivore.

The numbers of coyotes killed might be astonishing to some. In a seminal work, Fox and Papouchis (2005) estimated that over 500,000 coyotes are killed annually in the United States—a statistical trend that is echoed in Canada. That translates to a kill rate of at least one coyote per minute. The trend shows little abatement despite public backlash. In 2009 alone approximately 70,000 coyotes were killed in Saskatchewan, alongside several thousand in Ontario and Nova Scotia during government-sanctioned bounties (Alexander and Quinn 2012). In tandem, dozens of coyote bodies were found dumped in Alberta—ears cut off and reportedly taken into Saskatchewan to be cashed in illegally for the $20 bounty (Alexander and Quinn 2012). Disturbing as it may be to someone who cares for animals, the magnitude of these kills should not come as a surprise. Most provinces consider coyote a pest species, have no limits to killing, and do not legally require citizens to report killing coyotes (Alberta Environment and Sustainable Resource Development 2012). More difficult to grasp, perhaps, are the inhumane ways in which coyotes are killed or treated. They are shot, trapped, poisoned with strychnine, and sometimes just wounded for sport; coyotes are also hung upside down and dead from fence posts "to teach other coyotes a lesson to stay away." The motivations for such human behaviour are not well understood, but in their worst manifestations are obviously perverse.

Our contemporary relationship with coyote is made more challenging by the fact that they have learned to live among us humans in ways we seemingly had never imagined possible. Their heightened adaptive capacity conferred by a million years of evolution and fine tuning to our North American environment means that coyotes can survive almost anywhere—from the desert, to lush forests, and into the densest of urban cities. Unfortunately, by "setting up shop" in cities, coyote has confronted our average sensibility of which species belong in the wild and which belong in the city. Calgary—A City of Animals—exists mostly in the Foothills Parkland Natural Region—an area that has and will always be home to coyote. In this space, people have argued they see more coyotes because coyotes are expanding in numbers and have invaded our city. Evidence I have found reading from all types of sources, from early explorers' journals to Aboriginal stories to contemporary science, suggests that the rate of interaction has actually increased because human numbers have swelled in tandem with an expansion of our city footprint into coyote's sacred spaces. Recognizing and reconciling ourselves to the reality that we have borrowed coyote habitat may be one necessary shift toward realizing Calgary as a City of Animals.

Likewise, my research has led me to believe that our relationship to coyote reflects a dissonance in our choices around greener cities. Some people describe a desire for green spaces and a love of the attending biodiversity, such as the riverside parks and protected ravines in Calgary. Yet those same people sometimes do not want coyotes in those spaces. Even though we know the predator is essential to urban biodiversity, it is not welcome to intrude in these private spaces (e.g., our backyard or ravine) or to injure or kill our most precious belongings (e.g., pets), despite the fact that this is all appropriate behaviour for any coyote. Wild behaviour in the city seems to be misunderstood as incorrect behaviour, for the simple reason that it is happening in the city. But coyote has no concept of urban and rural etiquette. This presents obvious challenges to achieving the City of Animals. It forces us to answer tough questions: What behaviours will we tolerate, which species will we allow to live with us, how many can live in our shared urban spaces, and under what circumstances do we silence song dogs? In total, a City of Animals that includes coyotes leaves us to re-conceive of a moral compass that can adequately guide these relationships. We do not have a clearly articulated ethical framework to attend to the liminal species, such as habituated coyotes: they are neither fully wild nor fully domestic. Our existing ethical frameworks might help us make decisions about when to end a domestic animal's life based on compassion or unacceptable levels of aggression within the human framework. But what do we make of a wild animal, with ephemeral dependence upon humans, that becomes aggressive toward people in the city? When or what behaviours are un-wild enough that it appropriate to choose its fate? A vision of the City of Animals might include moral consideration for animals despite their position on the domestic-to-wild spectrum. It is increasingly apparent that this new vision requires understanding coyote ecology as well as human attitudes, beliefs, and behaviour toward the species (Treves and Bruskotter 2014).

we understand coyote ecology in the city

Coyote is distributed from California to Newfoundland, and from Alaska and the Canadian Northwest Territories to as far south as Panama. Evolution has conferred adaptive capacities that allow coyotes to exploit most habitats, including cities. Coyote ecology in cities is pretty easy to understand: if there is food and shelter—even if it's a garbage can and a culvert—and minimal threats, coyotes will persist and reproduce. While they likely are living an impoverished life in the city—not unlike that of someone forced to live on the street after living in a house –they persist: they live. Sadly, when confronted with regular human food attractants, individual coyote behaviour may change and they can become food conditioned and act aggressively toward people.

Quite fortunately in Calgary, coyotes consume a largely natural diet of small mammals, fruits, and other vegetation. However, they also eat human source foods (e.g., bird seed, crabapples, and garbage). While the procurement of human food is not surprising, the amount of scats containing human food may be cause for concern: in one study, one in six scats contained detectible garbage (Lukasik and Alexander 2012). And, while scant, approximately 1.5 per cent of scats contained pets (cat and dog). Avoiding conflict in a

Coyote pelts obtained by Harty boys, Tagona area, Alberta, 1910s, Glenbow Archives, NA-2616-23, Calgary, AB.

City of Animals would involve reducing access to these food sources (i.e., attractants). For instance, policy or law requiring the removal of any bird seed or fallen fruit from trees would be a recommended choice to improve successful sharing of the city. Interestingly, in an image submitted to us two years after the above study by a concerned citizen (Figure 1), coyote pointed out the severe limitations of our human imagination.

Despite conflicts and negative public sentiment, coyote's critical role in maintaining urban ecosystem function has been established by several scientific studies (Crooks and Soule 1999; Bekoff and Gese 2003). For example, coyotes can help maintain breeding and migratory bird populations by preying upon smaller carnivores such as feral cats (Crooks and Soule 1999), and they can control some prey populations such as white-tailed deer, gophers, and Canada geese. Hence, the City of Animals that includes coyotes also supports biodiversity. Assuming attractants are managed, a city that maintains green spaces (ravines, parks, riverways) where coyotes may be observed and appreciated at a safe distance, and a city that requires humans to be vigilant of their domestic animals, is a City of Animals that should, for the most part, allow humans and coyotes to co-flourish.

why not co-flourish?

By using the term *co-flourish*, I want to impart the notion that we can do more than simply enough to co-exist. To co-exist implies we live together in one space. Perhaps we need to push the envelope further? Why not co-flourish—why not coyotes and people co-creating new experiences that make better lives for both? A City of Animals might employ best practices and lead to a situation where we all benefit. This would require some effort to formulate a vision of how that might look on the ground. Do we have special spaces just for coyote? Can we create spaces where people who love coyotes benefit from interactions?

What are some things that block us realizing this goal? To begin, coyotes in the city confront our beliefs about where species belong. Coyotes are typically understood to be wild animals that belong in the wild areas. This idea is attributed to Philo and Wilbert (2000), who describe that people's relationships to animals organized by conceived "zones of human settlement" (city, agricultural, hinterland). Thus, cities tend to be viewed as spaces where domestic animals like dogs and cats mingle, agricultural areas on the perimeter of the city are where livestock belong, and the hinterland—beyond the agricultural zone—is where wild animals live. There are obvious inadequacies with this notion in practice, but it seems logical that this ideal underlies why people react so badly to the presence of coyotes in cities. Challenges to co-flourishing may rest largely on unarticulated concept of place, which may then inform our beliefs and behaviours toward coyotes. In a media content analysis (Alexander and Quinn 2012) and in current interviews conducted by the Foothills Coyote Initiative, the following juxtaposed statements convey some of the beliefs about coyote in the city (www.ucalgary.ca/canid-lab):

> "This is our home not theirs . . . coyotes are invading the city"

> "Coyotes were here first"

> "It's OK for them [coyotes] to kill a rabbit out in the wild but we shouldn't have to watch that in the city"

> "Live and let live . . . but I'd need to kill it if it came in the yard or hung around my animals"

> "You have to keep the balance of nature—don't kill coyotes, they keep the balance"

> "You have to keep the balance of nature—it is important to kill coyotes or the ecosystem will go out of balance"

> "I'm afraid to go outside, I shouldn't have to live like this"

> "If a coyote killed my animals, I would feel like I failed —failed my animals and the coyote"

Reflections upon the situation of coyotes in the city, if uninformed, can lead to belief that coyotes pose a risk to humans, then feelings that we or our loved ones (including pets) are in danger, followed by behaviour of killing coyotes to mitigate perceived risk. Yet the risk is extremely low. Correcting perceptions through education may be a necessary component of the City of Animals. But what do we know of this risk right now? My previous research showed that on average three people per year were reportedly bitten or scratched (i.e., attacked) by coyotes in Canadian urban centres (Alexander and Quinn 2011). These findings are consistent with the US statistics. Pets are killed by coyotes, but not as frequently as we imagine. Small dogs are at the greatest risk, in part because they are small and in part because they look like prey to a coyote. Notably, while some small dogs were killed in their yards, over 50 per cent of those attacks were interrupted when a person intervened by going into the yard and yelling or throwing things at the coyotes, and the dogs survived despite these being predatory events. Recent interviews conducted for the Foothills Coyote Initiative have reported similar findings. Yelling at coyotes, though not a recommended daily activity, is often enough to send them running and stop the predation of a domestic animal at critical times, such as when your animal is being attacked. Another way to minimize chances of attack is to become aware of your environmental and the coyote life cycle, and be vigilant during these times. For example, Lukasik and Alexander (2011) identified three key conflict drivers in Calgary, and these are largely driven by coyote ecology:

> Coyote conflict reports were significantly higher during the pup-rearing season (April–June) and the dispersal period (September–November).

> Neighbourhoods with ravines, river valleys, or small green spaces experienced higher conflict.

> Higher rates of conflict were associated with areas in which coyotes ate more garbage.

Coyotes can be more aggressive in particular during the denning season. At this time, coyotes are more likely to protect pups and act defensively or offensively toward densite intrusions. The general descriptions of behaviour and wounds inflicted by coyotes during these altercations are consistent with territorial fights between coyotes. Hence, there is strong evidence that if people are vigilant, engaged, and take precautions to leash their dogs and stay out of denning areas then the chance for conflict or attack could be dramatically reduced, thereby avoiding the routine killing of coyotes.

why not kill?

The trouble with killing as a management technique or to control coyote behaviour is primarily that it has been shown for years to be ecologically destructive and ineffective (Crabtree and Sheldon 1999). The higher kill rate can result in a younger and younger population of coyotes (Treves and Naughton-Treves 2005). And while populations of resilient species like coyotes may rebound quickly, this regrouping is generally accompanied by the breakdown of social structure, more breeding by younger individuals, and stifling of cross-generational teaching that may be helping to mitigate attacks by coyotes on people, pets, and livestock. The scientific evidence shows that killing leads to more solitary transient individuals entering areas that previously had stable packs, and these poorly educated, younger animals may be more prone to develop dependencies on human foods or develop "risky behaviours" like killing pets and livestock (Fox and Papouchis 2005; Shivik, Treves and Callahan 2003). Gordon Haber, who spent over forty-three years observing wolves in Alaska, spoke out for decades against the contemporary practice of killing for management (which usually prescribes killing 50–70 per cent of the population per year). Haber argued that managing wild canids by determining acceptable numbers to kill affronts our knowledge that each wolf is an individual and an important family member with particular social roles.

your calgary—a city of animals

We need to find a better solution than killing, and we must dream big. I know that living in a City of Animals will be worth it, but recognize that it will test our boundaries—perhaps beyond what we humans will be willing to concede. I believe our challenge is to push beyond co-existence and to co-flourish. If your City of Animals aims to be biodiverse then our collective understanding of predators (coyotes, owls, skunks, among others) needs to be recrafted. To truly be a City of Animals will require accepting unpleasant ecological realities, such as:

> when your domestic animal leaves the safety of your home it becomes part of the food chain

> when you enter the private spaces of a coyote you might be bitten

> aggression is natural, evolved, and necessary for coyotes

> we can mitigate being the target of aggression by controlling our attractants and being vigilant about pets

> coyotes (like all non-human animals) are just living; humans construct conflict.

Somewhere right now a coyote lies in silence, dead, after writhing in futile anguish for hours against a leghold trap. Chances are that in the time you finish reading this paper, another twenty have died; perhaps because of having killed a beloved pet dog or nipped somebody's hand—perhaps just because they were coyotes. Killing coyotes is not a requirement, it is a choice. It is Your City of Animals—Your Choice.

Coyote head, Calgary, Alberta. Glenbow Archives, NC-34-8, Calgary, AB.

works cited

Alberta Environment and Sustainable Resource Development. 2012. Alberta Guide to Hunting Regulations. http://www.albertaregulations.ca/huntingregs/gameregs.html.

Alberta Wildlife Act. (2014). http://www.qp.alberta.ca/documents/Regs/1997_143.pdf . Accessed September 7, 2014

Alexander, S.M., and M.S. Quinn. 2011. "Coyote (*Canis latrans*) Interactions with Humans and Pets Reported in the Canadian Print Media (1995–2010)." *Human Dimensions of Wildlife* 16: 345–59.

———. 2012. "Portrayal of Interactions between Humans and Coyotes (*Canis latrans*): Content Analysis of Canadian Print Media (1998–2010)." Special Issue: Urban Predators. *Cities and the Environment* 4(11): Article 9.

Bekoff, M., and E.M. Gese. 2003. "Coyote (Canis latrans)." In Wild Mammals of North America: Biology, Management, and Conservation, edited by G.A. Feldhamer, B.C. Thompson, and J.A Chapman, 467–81. Baltimore, MD: Johns Hopkins University Press.

Crabtree, R.L., and J.W. Sheldon. 1999. "Coyotes and Canid Coexistence in Yellowstone." In *Carnivores in Ecosystems: The Yellowstone Experiences*, edited by T.W. Clark, A.P. Curlee, S.C. Minsta, and P.M. Kareiva, 127–63. New Haven, CT: Yale University Press.

Crooks, K.R., and M.E. Soulé. 1999. "Mesopredator Release and Avifaunal Extinctions in a Fragmented System." *Nature* 400: 563–66.

Foothills Coyote Initiative, www.ucalgary.ca/canid-lab.

Fox, C.H., and C.M. Papouchis. 2005. *Coyotes in Our Midst: Coexisting with an Adaptable and Resilient Carnivore*. Animal Protection Institute, Sacramento. 64 pp.

Lukasik, V., and S. Alexander. 2011. "Human-Coyote Interactions in Calgary, Alberta." *Human Dimensions of Wildlife* 16(2): 114–27.

———. 2012. "Spatial and Temporal Variation of Coyote (*Canis latrans*) Diet in Calgary, Alberta." Special Issue: Urban Predators. *Cities and the Environment* 4(11). http://digitalcommons.lmu.edu/cate/vol4/iss1/8/.

Philo, C., and C. Wilbert. 2000. "Animal Spaces, Beastly Places: An Introduction." In *Animal Spaces, Beastly Places: New Geographies of Human-Animal Relations*, edited by C. Philo and C. Wilbert, 1–34. London: Routledge.

Shivik, J.A., A. Treves, and P. Callahan. 2003. "Nonlethal Techniques for Managing Predation: Primary And Secondary Repellents." *Conservation Biology* 17(6): 1531–37.

Treves, A., and J. Bruskotter. 2014. "Tolerance for Predatory Wildlife." *Science* 344 (6183): 476–77.

Treves, A., and Naughton-Treves. 2005. "Evaluating Lethal Control in the Management of Human-Wildlife Conflict." In *People and Wildlife: Conflict Or Coexistence*, edited by R. Woodruff, S. Thirgood, and A. Rabinowitz, 86–106. Cambridge, UK: Cambridge University Press..

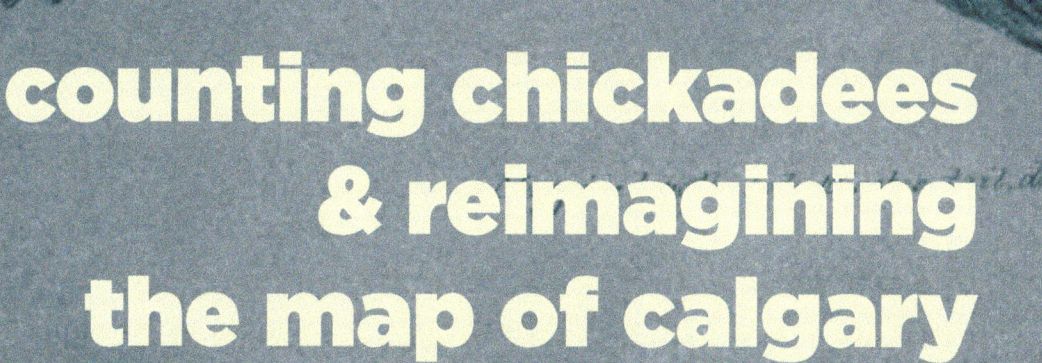

counting chickadees
& reimagining
the map of calgary

angela waldie

On the first day of each month, a small group of Calgarians gathers in the parking lot of Stanley Park to embark on the Elbow River Bird Survey. The meeting time varies with the season, as this walk usually starts an hour after sunrise. Gus Yaki and his wife, Aileen Pelzer, began this monthly ritual in July 1993 when they walked from Stanley Park, near their home, to the Glenmore Dam and realized a monthly survey of the birds along this route would offer valuable data on the changes in species from season to season and year to year. Like many citizen science projects, this initiative is valuable not only for the data it provides but also for the educational opportunities it offers. By guiding this walk for the past twenty-three years, Yaki and Pelzer have offered new and experienced birders the chance to learn more about the species that inspirit our city.

Yaki is a lifelong naturalist whose interest in birds began on his walks to and from school near North Battleford, Saskatchewan. As he notes in an interview with Matthew Sim, he learned to identify birds at a young age:

> I don't ever remember not being interested in birds and nature. One of my first teachers had a little 3 x 6 inch bird booklet. Walking almost three miles to school, I would see a bird on its nest. At school, during recess, I would thumb through this little publication to find a matching description. On the way home, I would confirm that I had correctly identified it.

This interest in birds led Yaki to create and operate a tour company, called Nature Travel Service, which allowed him to introduce participants to wildlife in countries around the world. Through his travels, Yaki believes he has seen approximately 5,000 bird species, roughly half of those currently known worldwide (Sim 2012).

In 1983, Yaki organized a tour retracing the 50,000-kilometre journey that Roger Tory Peterson, then America's foremost birder, and James Fisher, his British counterpart, undertook in 1953.[43] Following Peterson and Fisher's route, Yaki led participants from Newfoundland along the eastern seaboard to the Florida Keys, west to San Diego, and north to Washington's Olympic Peninsula. They then flew north to conclude with a tour of Alaska, including the Pribilof Islands in the Bering Sea. Lyn Hancock, who participated

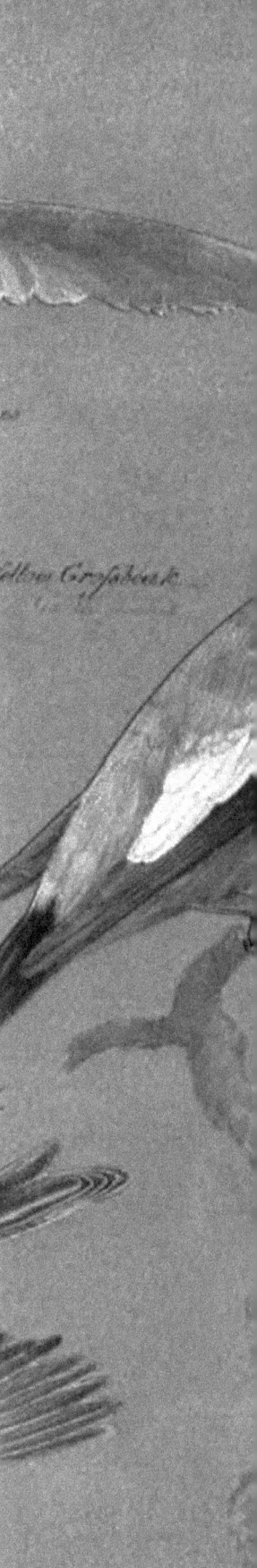

in this journey, documented it in *Looking for the Wild* (1986). Throughout this account, she describes Yaki as a tireless and enthusiastic guide, able to quickly read the details of the landscape and communicate them to his fellow travellers. She notes, for example, that "one time he was pointing out different ducks on the water with one hand, a warbler in the bush with the other, and at the same time motioning to his guests that there was a robin's nest in a tree above and a *Taraxacum officinale* plant on the ground" (Hancock 1986, xv). Yaki's keen eye and encyclopedic knowledge of species make him an ideal guide, and the pleasure he takes in sharing the wonders of his immediate environment is obvious on any tour one takes with him.

While the Elbow River Bird Survey spans approximately 5 kilometres rather than 50,000, Yaki leads it with the same enthusiasm he brought to the three-month trek around North America. His purpose also remains parallel: to instill an appreciation for other species and to observe how birds are impacted by human settlement. Writing about birdwatching in New York City, Jonathan Rosen (2008) suggests that in urban areas "the only remaining wild animals in abundance that carry on in spite of human development are birds" (5). Although some Calgarians may notice the squirrels, jackrabbits, deer, and coyotes with whom we share parts of the city, Rosen's point remains generally applicable to our urban experience. Birds are the most numerous and plentiful species we encounter in our yards, parks, and campuses, as well as on rivers and reservoirs. While many Calgarians pay little attention to such encounters and could name few of the bird species they see, others feed birds in their yards and visit natural areas in search of them. Some also seek the company of local experts, such as Yaki, to increase their knowledge of avian species.

Yaki begins each walk by asking for volunteers to keep track of the more plentiful species we will encounter, such as crows, ravens, magpies, Canada geese, mallards, robins, chickadees, and nuthatches. On a recent walk, with his characteristic playfulness, he also asked for a volunteer to count flamingos. Pelzer readily accepted this challenge, joking that these colourful lawn ornaments aren't as plentiful as they once were. In the four times I've participated in this walk, I've spent three of them counting black-capped chickadees—those friendly and charismatic birds that sometimes fly closer to greet us

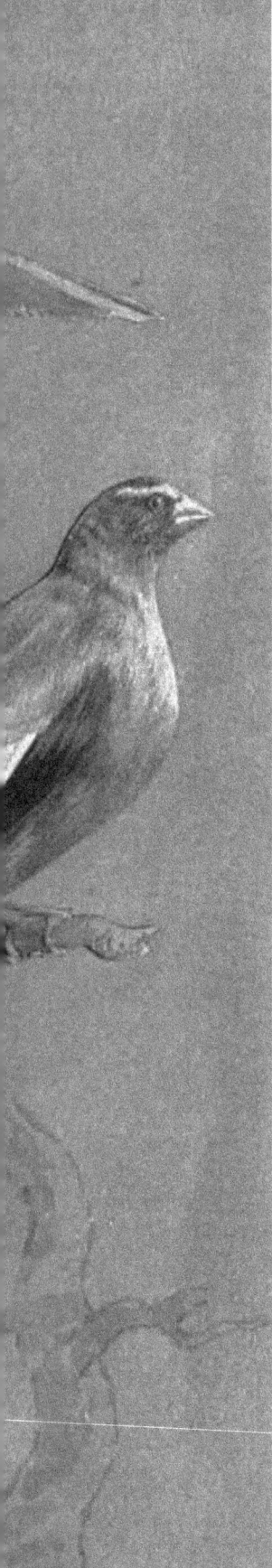

rather than flitting away. They are often heard before they are seen, and their companionable chatter prompts us to scan the nearby trees for these pulses of energy made animate. On the Elbow River Bird Survey, birds pre-empt conversation. The thread of a dropped conversation can always be picked up later, whereas the chatter of chickadees or the insistent *ank ank ank* of a red-breasted nuthatch demands immediate attention. The vocalizations of birds are often our best clue to their locations, and each call is followed by a collective effort to glimpse the elusive caller.

As Yaki's hearing has declined, he relies on participants to alert him to the audible clues the birds provide. Diane Stinson is a regular participant who has enthusiastically adopted this role. Stinson has been birding with Yaki for four years, and in that time she has learned to identify the songs and calls of a wide array of birds. As we traverse the route, I am amazed at her ability to isolate bird calls and identify their sources, a talent shared by other experienced birders who participate in this project. Their efforts are hindered in some areas, however, by construction and traffic noise. As Kathleen Dean Moore (2008) explains in her article "Silence Like Scouring Sand," human-made noise reduces viable habitat for other species by making it more difficult for them to communicate and remain alert to the dangers in their environments. For birds, vocalizations are often crucial to establishing territory and attracting mates. If males' mating calls are drowned out by noise, they will abandon potential nesting territory. The experience of trying to listen for birds in areas where traffic noise predominates reveals a hint of the challenges birds must face when trying to navigate the urban soundscape. Where the traffic of Elbow Drive rumbles across the river, I find myself straining to listen for bird calls above the constant din. If we cannot hear birds in this area, it is unlikely that they would be able to communicate with one another.

As the confluence of Elbow Drive and the Elbow River suggests, this walk includes areas to which birders would not typically be attracted. Although the route passes through a number of parks, it also includes streets where bird habitat has been fragmented by residential development. Moreover, the parks included along the route—Stanley Park, Riverdale Park, and Sandy Beach Park—do not include the large expanses of natural habitat found in areas such as the Weaselhead or Fish Creek Provincial Park. Stanley

Park, where the walk begins, is a multi-use suburban park just blocks from MacLeod Trail. It contains tennis courts and a swimming pool, and on warm days, the Elbow River Pathway through the park is filled with runners, cyclists, and dog walkers. In their midst, a group of birders carrying binoculars seems out of place, as though we are searching nostalgically for a landscape that is no longer there. It's encouraging that as we scan the slopes above the path, we find black-capped chickadees, red-breasted nuthatches, blue jays, and a northern flicker. Some of these birds flit back and forth across the water, taking advantage of whatever habitat they can find in the large backyards of the houses that line the river. A beaver lodge adjacent to a stone retaining wall is further evidence of the diversity of species that continue to subsist in this populated area.

The Elbow River Bird Survey offers a unique map that diverges from how most Calgarians experience this area. In a city where the majority of residents travel by car, this walk cuts across the typical routes used to get from one place to another. While the survey route mostly follows the Elbow River Pathway, it also extends to Riverdale Avenue and a few adjoining streets where there is no public access to the river. Along this route, Yaki has become familiar with the residents who feed the birds, and he occasionally instructs us to look into a yard to see what species have come to visit their feeders. At times it seems as though we are walking through Yaki and Pelzer's extended neighbourhood. They stop to talk with residents they know or wave to others who have grown accustomed to the spectacle of birders walking through their upscale urban neighbourhood on the first morning of each month. Residents sometimes mention notable species they have recently seen, such as a great horned owl or a bobcat. Although species not seen or heard during the monthly walk cannot be added to the count, reported sightings nevertheless help to broaden our understanding of the species that occupy these neighbourhoods, particularly the nocturnal ones that we're less likely to encounter during a morning walk.

Yaki, Pelzer, and the other participants in the Elbow River Bird Survey are engaged in an act of placemaking, layering this landscape with remembered moments and adding to our collective understanding of the value of the Elbow River to avian and other species. As Yi-Fu Tuan suggests in *Space and Place* (1977), "what begins as undifferentiated space becomes place as we get to know it better and endow it with value" (6).

The participants who retrace this route each month are compiling a map of shared memories. This is not a printed map or an electronic one, but rather an oral and kinesthetic map that one can best experience by participating in the walk. Yaki recalls a wintering population of wood ducks, peaking at thirty-nine individuals, which was part of a larger flock of ducks and geese attracted by an elderly couple who fed the waterfowl. Although they have since passed away and the birds no longer congregate along the river by the couple's former home, these winter flocks remain a vivid memory. Participants also share the memory of a leucistic robin[44] seen at the corner of 10th Street and Lansdowne Avenue SW. As the group of walkers shifts over time, those who have experienced unique sightings share their recollections, enlivening the journey with stories and expanding the realm of what might be seen. As we walk the pedestrian path between Lansdowne Avenue and Riverdale Park, we scan the trees for the great horned owls that have been seen here in past years. Each shadow among the branches seems momentarily animate, watching us with an air of possibility.

The map inscribed by the Elbow River Bird Survey is not limited to the route itself but is broadened by Yaki's knowledge of migration. At Sandy Beach, for example, he points out the nests of bank swallows, which winter as far south as Chile and Argentina. Even when these birds are not present, the far bank takes on a greater significance because of the life it supports in summer. Imagining the swallows' migration also heightens my understanding of the remarkable distances species travel between their breeding and wintering grounds and the importance of preserving habitat along this route. As we walk behind the fields of the Glenmore Athletic Park, Yaki points to an osprey nest atop one of the light standards. Because he watched the nest throughout the summer, he knows that the osprey pair successfully raised three young. He explains that they've likely migrated to Central or South America for the winter, but as osprey often return to the same nests, this one holds the promise of future arrivals and departures. In an age when many bird species are declining in numbers, ospreys are one of the rare good news stories. Since DDT was banned in 1972, populations of many birds of prey that were decimated by the pesticide have begun to recover. Yaki has noted a distinct increase in ospreys, bald eagles, and merlins since the Elbow River Bird Survey began.

In spite of some positive trends, however, many bird species are currently threatened by factors such as habitat loss, climate change, disease, and the introduction of invasive species. According to the *Partners in Flight (PIF) Landbird Conservation Plan 2016*, "the two most pervasive threats to landbirds in the U.S. and Canada are habitat loss due to urbanization and habitat degradation due to changing forest conditions" (14). Birds migrating through urban areas face a wide array of dangers, including habitat fragmentation and collisions with broadcast antennae and high-rise buildings, as well as predation by raccoons, house cats, chipmunks, magpies, crows, and other species that thrive around humans (Weidensaul 2000, 338–56). As Bridget Stutchbury (2007) explains in *Silence of the Songbirds*, migrating songbirds may stop in urban areas during their nocturnal migrations, either because of poor weather or because daylight has arrived. Often exhausted from their overnight flight, songbirds will seek shelter and food wherever they alight for the day (132). As stretches of viable stopover habitat are becoming more rare in urban areas, it is increasingly difficult for these birds to find the safety and sustenance they need.

In addition to species that migrate through cities, numerous species continue to breed in urban areas as long as sufficient habitat remains. However, since they began the Elbow River Bird Survey, Yaki and Pelzer have noticed the complete disappearance of some fifteen species that commonly bred along the route, including the Cooper's hawk, American kestrel, western wood-pewee, eastern kingbird, least flycatcher, ruby-crowned kinglet, song sparrow, Lincoln's sparrow, and Baltimore oriole. Yaki attributes their disappearance partly to the changing vegetation in the Elbow River Valley. Native plant species have increasingly been replaced by non-native species, which, as he explains, "have left all their bio-controls behind—their pathogens, parasites and predators" and which thrive as a result (personal communication). Not only do non-native species fail to support the insect populations that provide food for baby birds, they also tend to outcompete native species. A lack of food and increasingly fragmented habitat makes it difficult for birds to successfully raise young, resulting in the local extirpation of multiple species.

This bird walk is also a plant walk, as Yaki's knowledge of botany rivals his understanding of birds. As we leave Stanley Park, he points out Calgary's only black walnut tree. He also notes in October that the trees whose leaves remain green are non-native, attuned to habitats where winter arrives later. On one hand, this distinction may simply result in more varied foliage, but Yaki is a strong advocate for the importance of maintaining native species to support native bird populations. Along Riverdale Drive, he notes a bristle-cone pine and tells us of one in Nevada that is 5,700 years old. "Just imagine holding your limbs out for 5,700 years," he quips, holding out his arms. "I can't even hold mine out for 57 seconds." He points out a prominent burl in one tree and when I ask him whether it could cause the tree to die, he tells me, "probably not. It's been that way as long as I've known it." Although his verb choice in this statement may be accidental, it captures Yaki's relationship to the species he encounters along this walk. He *knows* them, not merely in the sense of knowing they are there, or being able to identify them, but as he might greet a friend he sees from time to time. They are residents of this neighbourhood just as the homeowners are.

Walking with Yaki reminds me of reading Aldo Leopold's *A Sand County Almanac* (1989), as he cultivates an attention to the natural world that rivals Leopold's descriptions of the lands surrounding his Wisconsin farm. Of the non-descript flower draba, Leopold writes:

> He who hopes for spring with upturned eye never sees so small a thing as Draba. He who despairs of spring with downcast eye steps on it, unknowing. He who searches for spring with his knees in the mud finds it, in abundance. (26)

Yaki searches for every season "with his knees in the mud," metaphorically at least, and generously shares his passion with whomever will follow. As we ascend from Sandy Beach to the last stretch of the walk, he points out, in spring, the pasqueflowers that are the first to bloom on a south-facing slope. Like Leopold, he notes the arrivals and departures of all species that characterize his home place, and the records he compiles from year to year provide a valuable archive of shifting patterns. As climate change threatens to disrupt the carefully tuned relationships on which many species rely, the records and reflections of citizen scientists will be increasingly valuable in pointing out subtle changes in the seasons.

The Elbow River Bird Survey ends at the Glenmore Dam, where various species of grebes, ducks, geese, or phalaropes can sometimes be seen. Although the walkers will return to the parking lot at the Sandy Beach dog park at 50th Avenue SW, where they have coordinated vehicles to transport participants back to Stanley Park, Yaki explains that no birds can be counted on the return unless they are from a species not yet seen that day. This ensures that the same birds are not counted twice. At the dam, the count ends with a collaborative list, a roll call of sorts, as Yaki records the birds seen and the number of individuals of each. As he calls out the species' names, each participant contributes the number of the species he or she has been assigned to count. This feels to me like a celebration of the diversity of species that have greeted us along the journey, a testament to those that continue to exist alongside us, in spite of noise pollution, the introduction of invasive species, and loss of habitat.

On each of the walks in which I've participated, the number of species recorded is far greater than what I would have identified alone, which emphasizes the importance of spending time with experienced birders. This number is lower, however, than the diversity of species Yaki has encountered here in the past, revealing that even the most observant birders cannot spot birds that no longer frequent this area. As I leave the group at the dam to continue on to my home in Lakeview, I walk with a heightened appreciation of the species that surround me. Walking along Glenmore Trail north of Rockyview Hospital, I am keenly aware that there are areas of the city where little exists but pavement, cars, and noise. A short distance from this thoroughfare, however, bird calls resume, and on recent walks home I have seen a bald eagle, flickers, robins, magpies, and chickadees. Sometimes I find myself absent-mindedly counting these natural companions before I realize this month's count is over. Although the data Yaki gathers provides an invaluable archive, I believe that the greatest benefit of his project is the awareness he cultivates. The Elbow River Bird Survey confirms that we have the privilege to share a city with species such as bald eagles, Townsend's solitaires, and yellow warblers. By encouraging us to listen to the avian voices that persist in urban areas, Yaki inspires us to advocate for those species that remain among us.

works cited

Hancock, Lyn. 1986. *Looking for the Wild: A 30,000-mile Naturalists' Journey Across North America*. Toronto: Doubleday Canada.

Leopold, Aldo. 1989. *A Sand County Almanac, and Sketches Here and There*. New York: Oxford University Press. First published 1949 by Oxford University Press.

Moore, Kathleen Dean. 2008. "Silence Like Scouring Sand." *Orion*. https://orionmagazine.org/article/silence-like-scouring-sand/.

Partners in Flight. 2016. *Partners in Flight Landbird Conservation Plan 2016*. http://www.partnersinflight.org/plans/landbird-conservation-plan/.

Rosen, Jonathan. 2008. *The Life of the Skies: Birding at the End of Nature*. New York: Farrar, Strauss and Giroux.

Sim, Matthew. 2012. "Famous Birders: Gus Yaki." *Birds Calgary*. 21 October. https://birdscalgary.wordpress.com/2012/10/21/famous-birders-gus-yaki/.

Stutchbury, Bridget. 2007. *Silence of the Songbirds: How We Are Losing the World's Songbirds and What We Can Do to Save Them*. New York: HarperCollins.

Tuan, Yi-Fu. 1977. *Space and Place: The Perspective of Experience*. Minneapolis: University of Minnesota Press.

Weidensaul, Scott. 2000. *Living on the Wind: Across the Hemisphere with Migratory Birds*. New York: North Point Press.

illustrations throughout article:
Painting of winter birds at Cumberland House. 1819-1820, Glenbow Archives, NA-132-2 & NA-132-3, Calgary, AB.

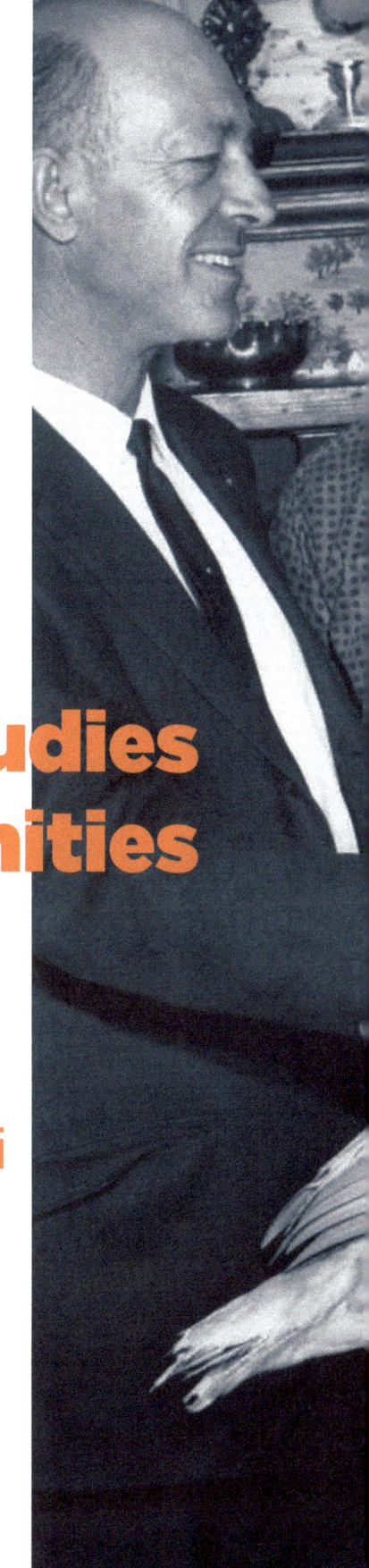

critical animal studies & the humanities

a critical introduction

mohammad sadeghi esfahlani

university of calgary

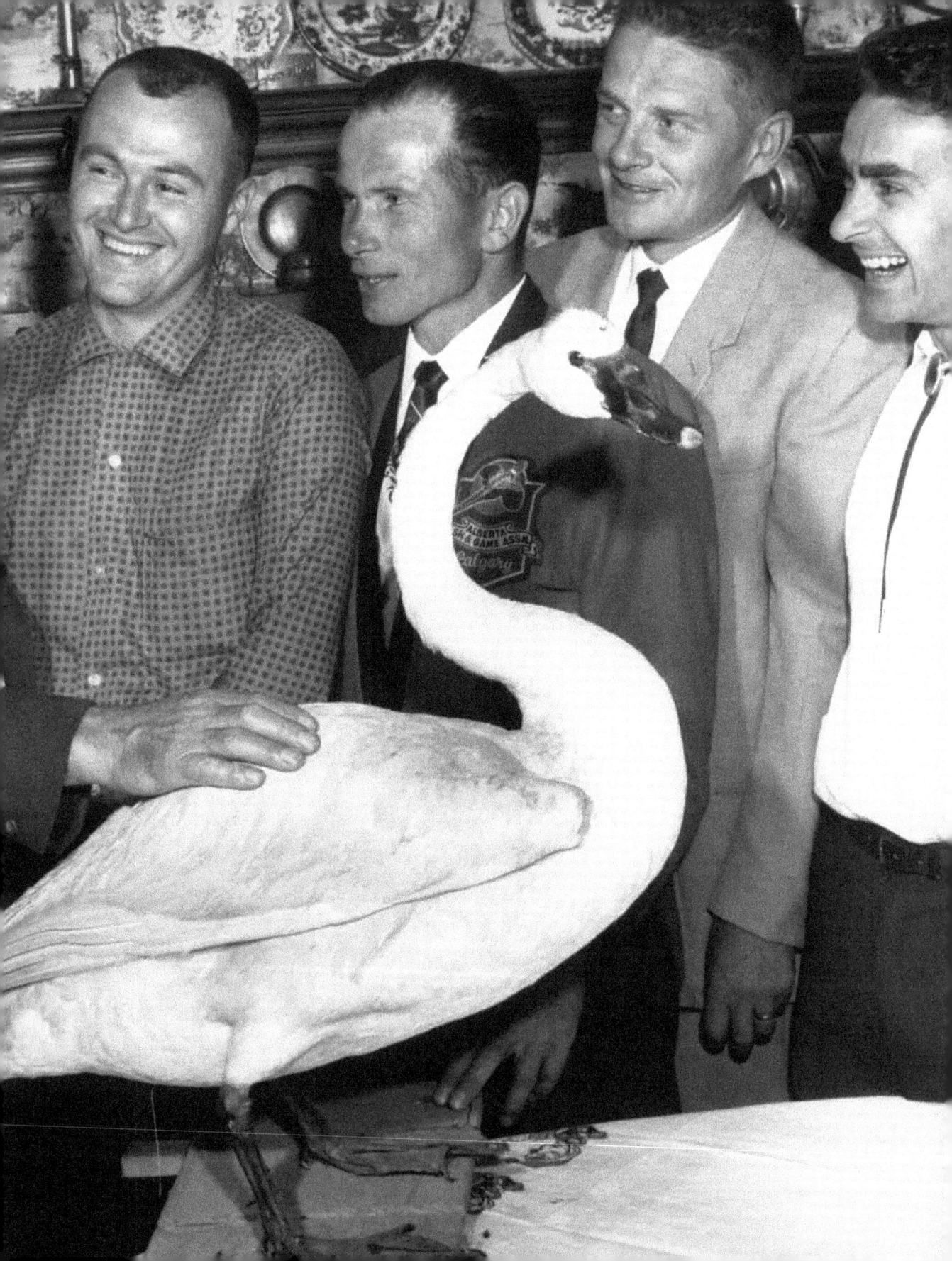

Acting as a project manager for the Calgary Institute for the Humanities, I managed the research and coordination involved in organizing the 34th Community Seminar in 2016. Since one of my tasks was to conduct background research in humanities literature concerning animals and our relationship with them, I welcomed this opportunity to contribute to this volume: this chapter will introduce the field of Critical Animal Studies and its relation to the humanities.

Critical Animal Studies is an interdisciplinary field of scholarship on the frontiers of the humanities. It is a remarkably radical field of thought and action, focused on understanding how oppression and different oppressive systems intersect, to overcome practices of exploitation and move toward a trans-species social justice.

In this chapter, I will introduce the progressive epistemological stance of Critical Animal Studies activist-scholars and their avant-garde approach to finding the roots of some of these profound issues and proposing radical solutions. However, I will also identify conceptual gaps and practical limits of the approaches advocated by Critical Animal Studies. The next section will describe the background of Critical Animal Studies and its development as a field of academic scholarship. The following section will illuminate the key issues and practical approaches in the literature. On this basis, I will highlight some of the gaps in the radical ideas and some of the limits of the practical approaches and will conclude by advocating for moderate efforts within institutional frameworks and radical efforts on a personal level to overcome such limits and gaps and facilitate social change.

the development of critical animal studies: background, scholarship & institutions

Critical Animal Studies departs from a fundamental assumption underlying Humanism, inherited in postmodern and post-humanist thought: Anthropocentrism, the assumption of human exceptionalism as a superior species. Anthropocentrism is rooted in dualist thinking and conceptual distinctions between Human/Animal and Civilization/Wilderness and, consequently, thinking of such things as species, races, and genders hierarchically. Critical Animal Studies scholars argue that this facilitates ideologies and practices of oppression and exploitation. Thus, Critical Animal Studies opposes dualist thinking and making distinctions between humans and animals as well as anthropocentric assumptions about the superiority of the human species.

Critical Animal Studies can be considered the scholarly manifestation of the confluence of animal liberation, advocacy, and rights movements, and the humanities. Although the

previous illustration:
Fish & Game Association hunter training, Calgary, Alberta. 1964, Glenbow Archives, PA-1599-258-8, Calgary, AB.

roots of Critical Animal Studies can be traced back to ancient Eastern religions and early Western philosophers such as Pythagoras (6th century BC), modern Critical Animal Studies criticizes the history of religious thought and philosophy as being dominated by anthropocentric views that legitimize hierarchization of living species and the domination of humans over animals; in particular, the idea of human "dominion," established by the "monotheistic powerhouse of Christianity" provides a "supernatural authorization for the exploitation" and provides the basis for certain mainstream ideologies in contemporary Western culture (Nocella II et al. xxi, xxii).

The philosophical cornerstone of the modern animal rights movement is Peter Singer's *Animal Liberation*, which is also the most acclaimed work of scholarship in Critical Animal Studies. Building upon the ideas of Jeremy Bentham—the founder of utilitarian philosophy who established principles such as happiness expectations and the capability for suffering as the basis for moral evaluations—Singer has particularly focused on the problem of animal suffering, arguing that actions become moral duties whenever collective benefits (happiness) outweigh costs (suffering). The most significant contribution of this work is the critical examination of the concept of speciesism: a hierarchical understanding of the value of species and the consequent morality that privileges a certain kind. He compares the underlying prejudice of speciesism to that of racism and sexism, similarly embedded and manifested in social institutions, practices, and relationships (Cudworth 25).

Contemporary Critical Animal Studies, however, is critical toward utilitarian assumptions: assuming that humans have moral superiority based on cognitive capabilities—particularly, the capability to contemplate and project their existence and desire into the future—is in line with the traditional moral hierarchy of humanist thought, which ultimately justifies exploitation (Steiner 82). Hence, modern Critical Animal Studies has a strong affinity with feminism, post-colonial theory, and particularly, with ecofeminist writings of the 1970s and 1980s (Taylor and Twine 5, 6; Sorenson xxi). It departs from Singer on practical solutions to the problem of animal suffering (such as offered by genetic engineering), since those solutions ignore the inherent value of an animal's "identity and beingness" (Davis 178–81). Rather, and in line with the critical tradition in the humanities and social sciences, "Critical Animal Studies rejects the humanist frame" (Taylor and Twine 7) in favour of a "total liberation frame": a theoretical objective of "activist-scholars"—"radical environmentalists"—to "holistically understand movements" that seek to eliminate all forms of oppression, prejudice, and discrimination and shift global consciousness toward "Social-Environmental-Species Justice" (Fitzgerald and Pellow 42–47). Particularly, the ecofeminist influence on Critical Animal Studies illuminates "how the material and symbolic exploitation of animals intersects with and helps maintain dominant categories of gender, race and class" (Taylor and Twine 4).

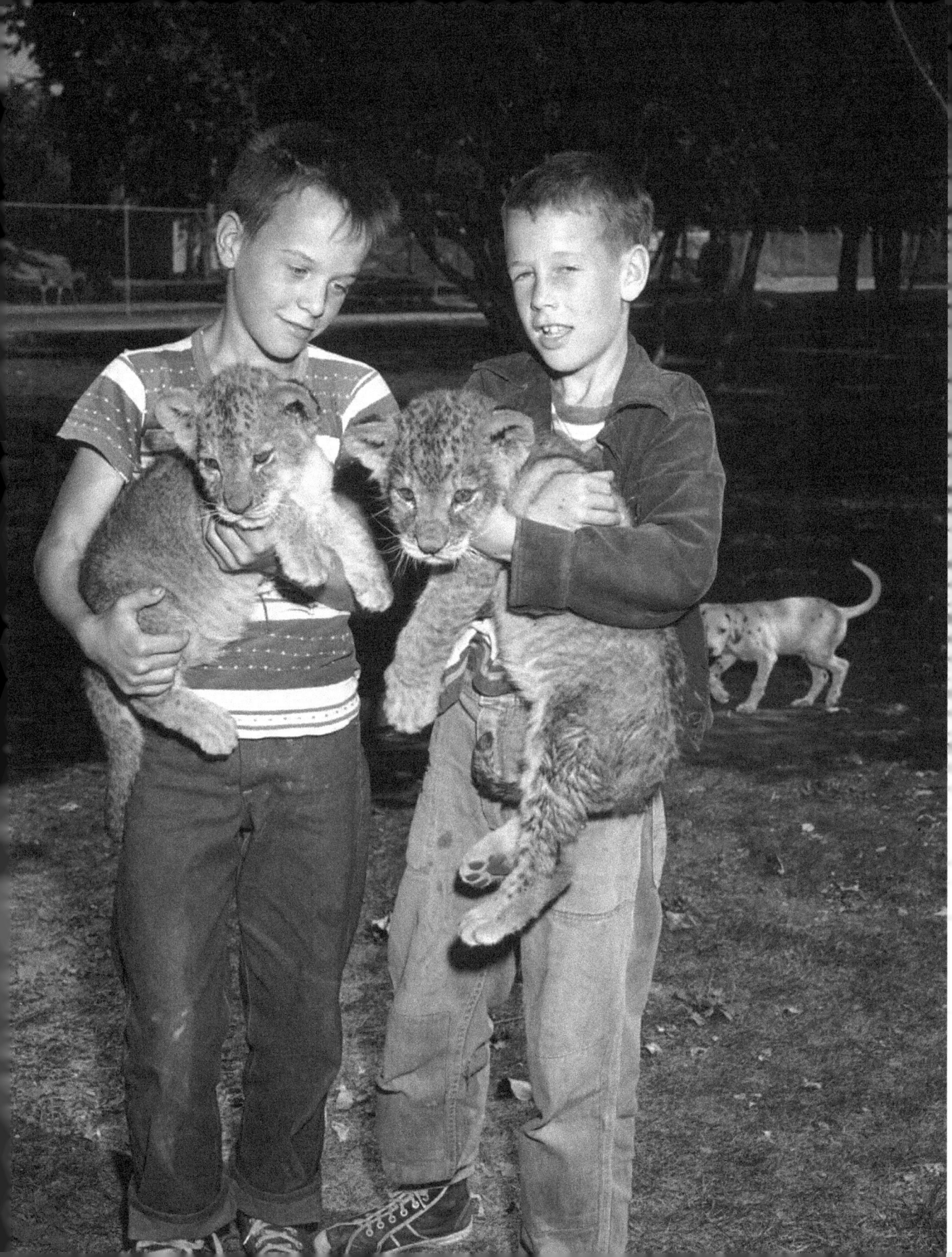

Current Critical Animal Studies scholars (Adams 21–26; Sorenson xxi) believe that since the agricultural revolution, the structural foundations of human society and the origins of human relations rest upon our oppressive and exploitative relationship with animals. In an effort to turn away from convictions that facilitate exploitation, they are committed to re-thinking the "boundaries and continuities between humans and other animals and our duties towards other beings," and taking into account the "animal standpoint" (Sorenson xx).

Critical Animal Studies discourse takes a sharply oppositional stance toward the field of Animal Studies in sciences—particularly the practice of vivisection and animal experimentation (Peggs 36)—and even toward humanities scholars who refer to Animal Studies rather than Human-Animal Studies or Critical Animal Studies, criticizing them for having no interest in taking the animal standpoint and investigating their oppression, exploitation, and liberation as a moral end in and of itself (Nocella II et al. xxiv). While the focus of Animal Studies is on the "question of the animal," Critical Animal Studies shifts the focus toward questioning the "conditions of the animal," with "a direct focus on the circumstances and treatment of animals." Hence, Critical Animal Studies seeks to shift the focus of the humanities from humans toward ecology and animal life (Taylor and Twine 2). This shift of focus has given Critical Animal Studies a critical edge in addressing current debates and urgent questions of our time, particularly by challenging traditional perspectives in the social and natural sciences and in spanning the boundaries of the humanities.

practical issues: problems & solutions

A central issue for Critical Animal Studies is how to engage theory directly and indirectly to achieve social change on both individual and institutional levels (Taylor and Twine 6). Faced with humanity's tremendous historic legacy of cruelty and exploitation—beginning with the original sin of animal oppression by humans—the approach of Critical Animal Studies calls for "a clear line of praxis"—"to professionalize, legitimize and prioritize an ethics theory in practice"—with a focus on avoiding harm to animals (Glaser and Roy 90–91). The "praxis" approach of Critical Animal Studies is based on the ethics of social and material veganism, directed against the central problem in the field: the Animal Industrial Complex (Stallwood 299).

A central premise of Critical Animal Studies scholarship is that "capitalist societies exist only in and through their exploitation of other animals" (Drew and Taylor 159). The notion of an Animal Industrial Complex is inspired by Eisenhower's Military-Industrial Complex and yet is construed to be the precedent of all capitalist systems (Fitzgerald and Pellow

40) in the sense that "animal exploitation . . . [is] central to systems of oppression" (Nocella II et al. xxi). The global Animal Industrial Complex is rooted in a long history of violence toward animals and Indigenous people by slaughterhouse operators in a quest for "private wealth accumulation"—a fundamental ideology of European colonialism and contemporary neo-liberal capitalism. In this context, Critical Animal Studies argues that the oppression and exploitation of devalued humans and animals are deeply entangled (Nibert 15–17).

Hence, the greater problem of Critical Animal Studies relates to the ideological paradigms of our time, particularly when it comes to "carnism" (meat eating ideology) and commodification of animals for human consumption, with tremendous institutional legacy representation through the Animal Industrial Complex (Fitzgerald and Pellow 40), including universities in which animals are used as objects of research for vivisection and experimentation (Sorenson xvii). Critical Animal Studies is framed both as a social movement and a moral crusade against the Animal Industrial Complex (Stallwood). Therefore, the engaged theory approach of Critical Animal Studies is a political-intellectual project to "understand society from the perspective of those who are oppressed and victimized and to engage in political action to protect them" (Sorenson xx). This goal is pursued by seeking to influence lifestyle choices on a personal level as well as to bring change to the realm of material institutions through the praxis of veganism (Weitzenfeld and Joy 25).

The road to salvation in Critical Animal Studies is the social and ethical praxis of veganism. Veganism provides a moral baseline for an anarchist, non-violent social movement based on "true compassion" that uses various strategies of bottom-up resistance against systems of domination. These strategies range from "taking it to the streets" and "public civil disobedience" (White and Cudworth 215) to public education campaigns (Stallwood 312) and innovative educational strategies to create a space and language in academia that facilitates an understanding of the "animal standpoint" (Linne and Pedersen 282). Vegan praxis seeks to challenge all oppressive power structures through an "ever-changing way of understanding and relating to oneself and all other beings based on the principles of true freedom— empathy, authenticity, reciprocity, justice and integrity" (Weitzenfeld and Joy 25).

The quest of veganism is deeply personal; it's a quest to mobilize knowledge in order to change deeply ingrained personal habits: "breaking with your formal self" (Salih 61), not only when it comes to eating meat but rather in all consumption. It is suggested that vegans, unless brought up so, will most probably have undergone a sort of "breakdown" or "breakthrough" in their lives that has fundamentally changed their world view. Hence, being vegan means that as the first step toward ethical consumption, one must "refuse to accept what is presented to you," break down products to their constituent parts and subject them to ethical scrutiny. On the downside, since we are living in a world of institutionalized capitalist markets, intensive and repeated breakdowns can lead to cognitive dissonance and dismay and, ultimately, to marginalization and social exclusion (Salih 62). But veganism is neither supposed to be a (counter-) ideology nor "a match for the Animal Industrial Complex" (Stallwood 298), but rather, the capacity of the self-disrupting mind to break down and open itself to new possibilities. Veganism has no rules, only some "perceived wrongs" (Salih 64–65).

limits & gaps

Ultimately, the purpose of all forms of life is sustenance. On the other hand, living beings nourish themselves on the dead, both literally in biological terms and metaphorically in terms of inheriting the legacy of the dead's existence. If we are to take our subjective sense of compassion to its "true" end and want to wage a "moral crusade" on behalf of beings that our form of consciousness can empathize with, as some Critical Animal Studies scholars suggest (Stallwood 314), are we not assuming some sort of "exceptionalism" for our existence? Hence remains the question: What are the limits of our compassion? Where are we supposed to draw the lines for understanding biological life as our subject of compassion?

Veganism does not offer any rules or systematic ideology; it merely seeks to raise consciousness by encouraging the idea of overcoming one's self. Hence, there seems to be a considerable gap in terms of what shall count as the subject of our empathy, compassion, and ethics and where we can draw limits; at least a systematic debate about these fundamental questions seems to be missing from contemporary Critical Animal Studies literature. Especially when considering emerging developments in the food industries such as entomophagy and vitro meat, these conceptual gaps may also explain the lack of a response of Critical Animal Studies toward such developments and emerging issues.

Entomophagy is the human practice of eating insects. Despite its roots in various cultures around the world, it has emerged as a new trend in response to the major global problem of food insecurity. Most recently, a spin-off start-up formed at McGill University's management program won the Clinton Global Initiative's HULT prize competition for its business model on insect farming.[45] Insect farming produces significantly lower greenhouse gas emissions than the farming of animals by the Animal Industrial Complex and, in addition to food insecurity, responds to other problems such as water security and global warming as well. Whereas the most recent issue of the *Animal Studies Journal*[46] is dedicated to the subject of insects, Critical Animal Studies has yet to respond to this trend. In this case, taking the "animal standpoint" seems like a difficult riddle:

next illustration:
Conservative women's club tea, Calgary, Alberta. 1941, Glenbow Archives, PA-1599-192-29, Calgary, AB.

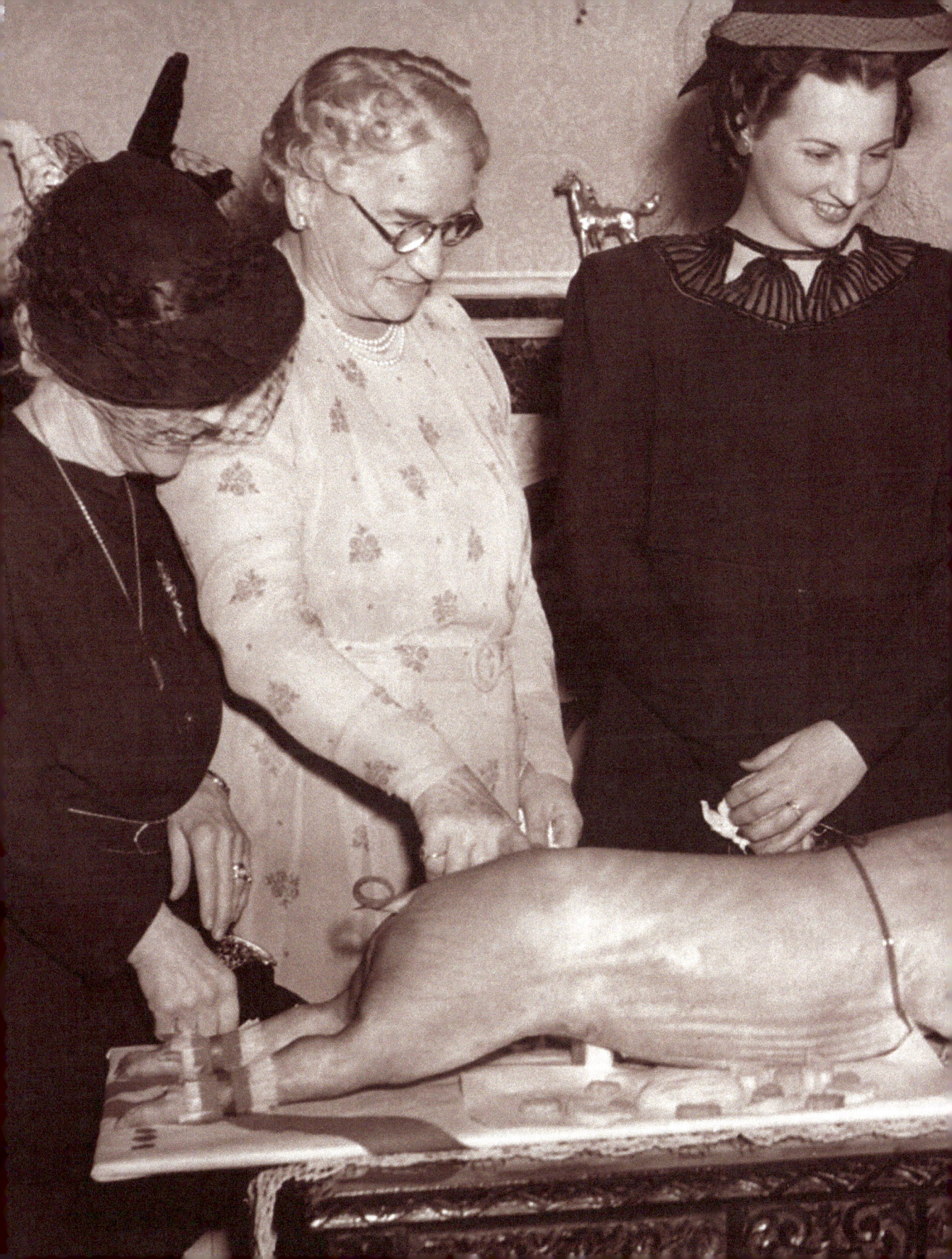

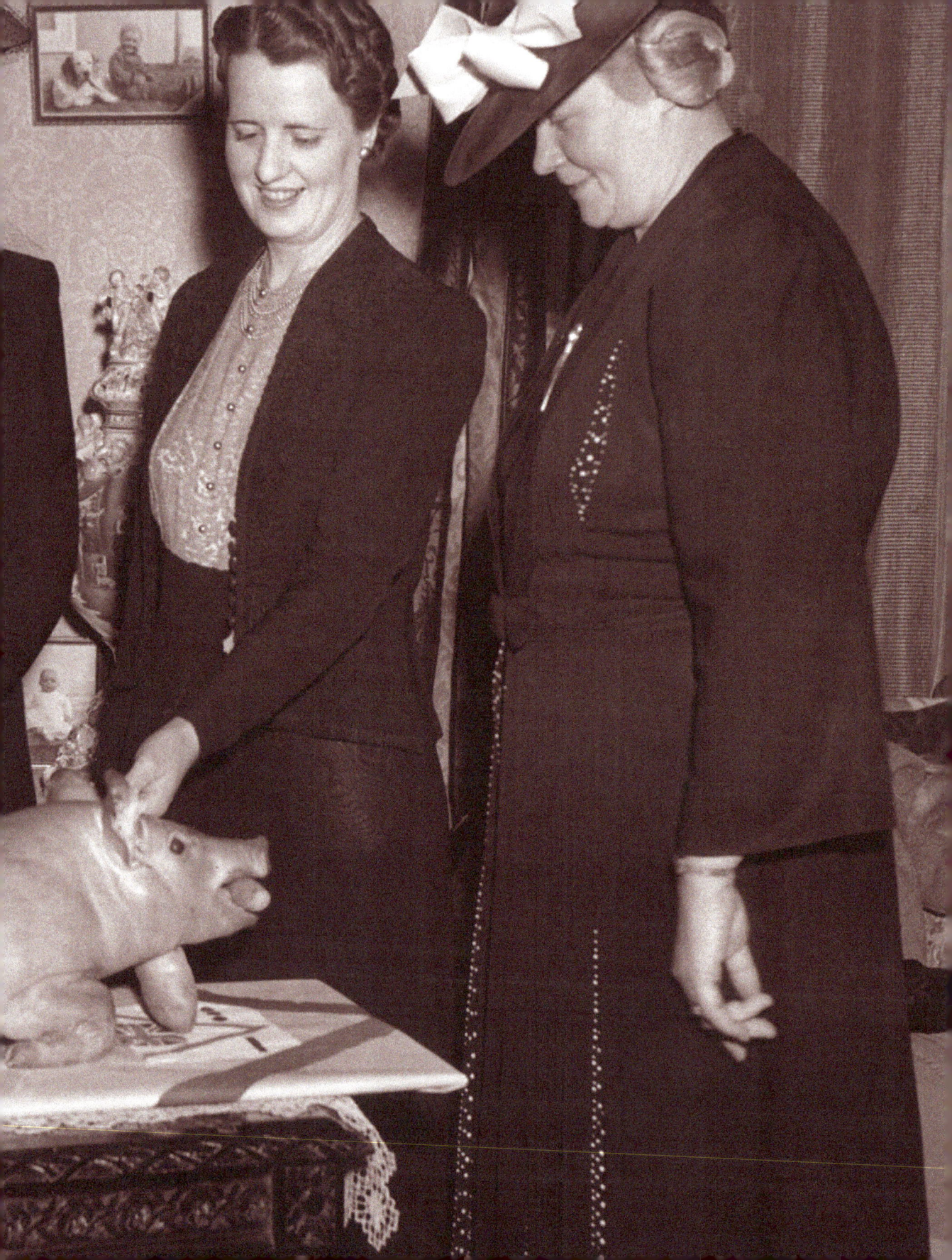

Shall we have compassion for mealworms, crickets, and cockroaches? For that end, can we empathize with such an existence and take its point of view? How? If one is going this far for "true" compassion, would it be worth going further and empathizing with the plant which is determined to grow further each and every day?

Speaking of everlasting growth, since the very concept of capitalism seems to be a central subject of criticism in Critical Animal Studies, an ethical debate about solutions which have somewhat overcome the animal question seems to be missing as well: for instance, vitro meat is emerging as a technology for producing muscular tissues cultured in the lab,[47] advanced plant-based meat imitations such as those produced by "Impossible Foods" (www.impossiblefoods.com) are introduced to global markets, and engineered food replacements such as "Soylent" offer a GMO-based vegan food to eradicate the human problem of nutrition altogether. How shall these products be considered ethically, given that they result from economic entrepreneurship and venture capitalism rather than a value-based community culture? Does the very act of market participation not empower capitalism as the umbrella ideology presiding over all current systems of oppression?

Finally, if the practice of eating meat is responsible for so much of our ideological and historic legacy and, to some accounts, for the biological possibility of our existence,[48] why are we obligated to repudiate and condemn it as the original sin that enabled our becoming? Why shall we, in exception to all other species, commission ourselves with preserving life from death? If so, does this not parallel the approach of Christianity and similar religious ideologies in terms of assuming human exceptionality while paradoxically denouncing the origins of its exceptional existence?

conclusions

One of the key programs of the Calgary Institute for the Humanities is knowledge engagement.[49] With this goal in mind, I managed the 34th Annual Community Seminar and acted on behalf of the institute in bringing together humanities scholars and the local community to explore Calgary from the "animal standpoint." Whereas the subjects revolved around the history of human-animal relationship in the Canadian urban context and particularly the city of Calgary, this year's community seminar had an interesting side effect; after initial doubts about offering the right proportion of vegan food—ordered at a local "ethical vegetarian" restaurant—participants overwhelmingly went for the vegan option.[50]

On the other hand, the City of Calgary recently published its 10-year biodiversity strategic plan, which aims to "provide a comprehensive and systematic approach to protect-

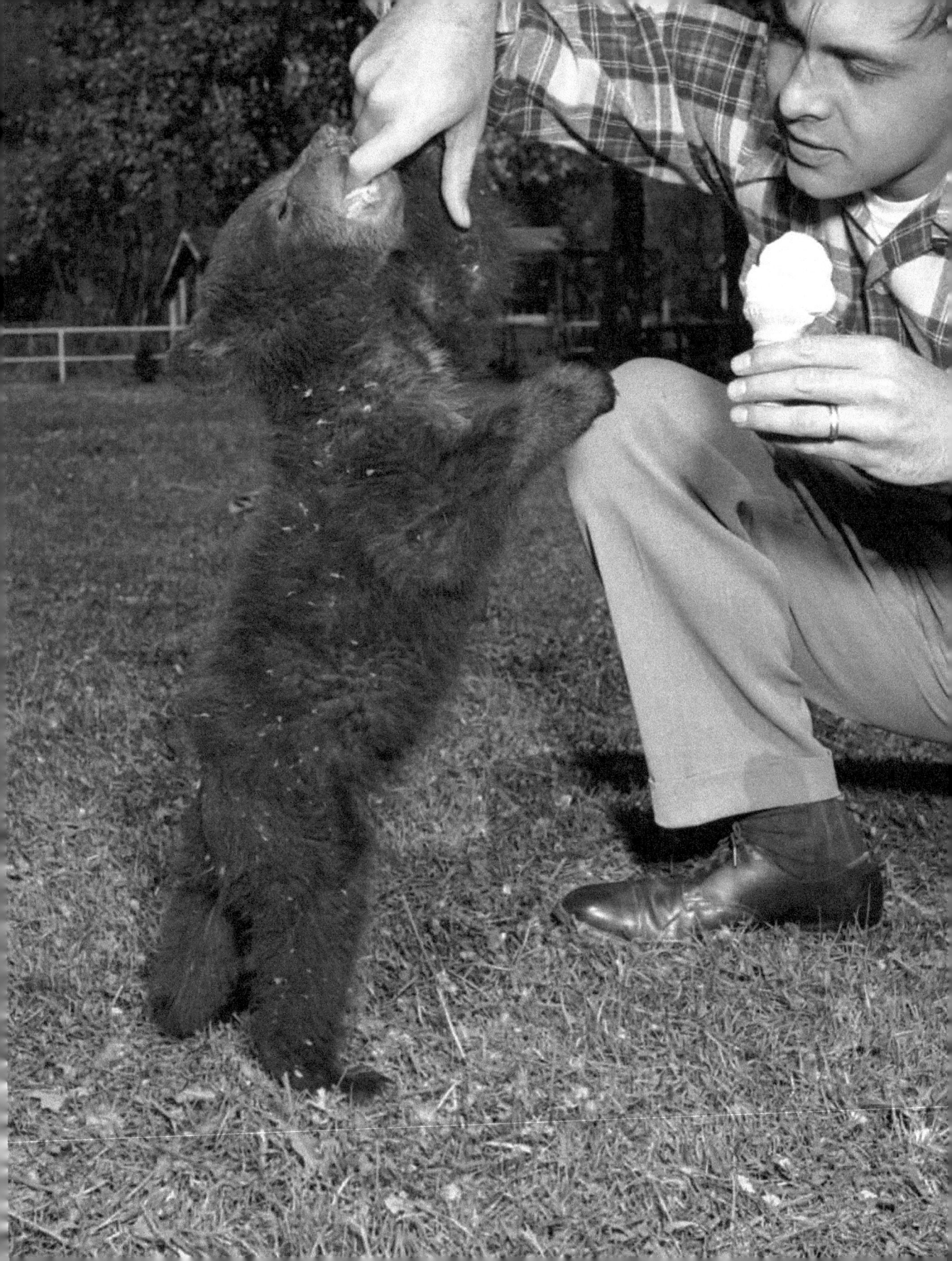

ing, developing and managing its natural and built environments for healthy ecological processes in support of biodiversity." To this end, this plan envisions the revival of Calgary's diversity and richness in wildlife, vegetation, and landscape. Negotiated by active citizens and enacted by Calgary's city council, this plan overwhelmingly resonated with seminar participants but also raised critical questions.

Hence, moderate efforts can prove to be an effective alternative to radical activism for bringing about change; especially when faced with persistent legacies, opportunities within institutional frameworks can be utilized to facilitate incremental change. A realistic hope for universal change from a strictly anarchist perspective would rely on catastrophes and, in the ideal situation, result in an immediate, tremendous destruction of all institutional frameworks. Hence, renceadicalism might be worth exploring on a personal level, but on a social and institutional level, radical approaches can come at a cost that is irresponsible to assume on behalf of others.

Personally, engaging with the Critical Animal Studies Scholarship did in fact "disrupt" me toward contemplating veganism. My reluctance toward eating meat increased drastically enough that I actively began seeking alternatives. Faced with problems such as breaking habits, having no access to affordable vegan food or a "space" that allows and promotes a vegan lifestyle on the University of Calgary campus, and while having to function in a competitive academic environment that leaves little "time" for a vegan lifestyle, I found a radical solution: "Soylent"—an open source, GMO-based vegan meal replacement, engineered to provide optimal nutrition, produced by a crowd-funded start-up.[51]

Experimenting with radical diet change such as "going Soylent" might be fraught with risk, particularly given the fact that any kind of research about the effects of this kind of food on the human body and psyche is missing at this point. However, I hope that exploring radicalism on a personal level can open up a new perspective for gaining and sharing an interesting experience of self-disruption. Perhaps such experiential accounts can open a critical perspective to the vegan discourse and disrupt its concepts, practices, and even its meaning. Perhaps it's now time for veganism to "break down" in order to "break through."

works cited

Adams, Carol. "The War on Compassion." In Sorenson, ed. 18–28.

Calarco, Matthew. *Thinking Through Animals: Identity, Difference, Indistinction*. Stanford, CA: Stanford University Press, 2015.

Cudworth, Erika. "Beyond Speciesism: Intersectionality, Critical Sociology and the Human Domination of Other Animals." In Taylor and Twine, eds. 19–35..

Davis, Karen. "Anthropomorphic Visions of Chickens Bred for Human Consumption." In Sorenson, ed. 169–85.

Drew, Lara, and Nik Taylor. "Engaged Activist Research: Challenging Apolitical Objectivity." In Nocella II et al., eds. 158–76.

Fitzgerald, Amy, and David Pellow. "Ecological Defence for Animal Liberation: A Holistic Understanding of the World." In Nocella II et al., eds. 28–48.

Glaser, Carol, and Arpan Roy. "The Ivory Trap: Bridging the Gap Between Activism and the Academy." In Sorenson, ed. 89–109.

Linne, Tobias, and Helena Pedersen. "'Expanding My Universe': Critical Animal Studies Education as Theory, Politics, and Practice." In Sorenson, ed. 268-83.

Nibert, David. "Animals, Immigrants and Profits: Slaughterhouses and the Political Economy of Oppression." In Sorenson, ed. 3–17.

Nocella II, Anthony J., et al., eds. *Defining Critical Animal Studies: An Intersectional Social Justice Approach for Liberation*. New York: Peter Lang, 2014.

Peggs, Kay. "From Centre to Margins and Back Again: Critical Animal Studies and the Reflexive Human Self." In Taylor and Twine, eds. 36–51.

Salih, Sara. "Vegans on the Verge of a Nervous Breakdown." In Taylor and Twine, eds.. 52–68.

Singer, Peter. *Animal Liberation: A New Ethics for Our Treatment of Animals*. New York: New York Review, 1975.

Sorenson, John, ed. *Critical Animal Studies: Thinking the Unthinkable*. Toronto: Canadian Scholars' Press, 2014.

Stallwood, Kim. "Animal Rights: Moral Crusade or Social Movement?" In Sorenson, ed. 298–317.

Steiner, Gary. "Animals as Subjects and the Rehabilitation of Humanism." In Sorenson, ed. 79–92.

Taylor, Nik, and Richard Twine, eds. *The Rise of Critical Animal Studies: From the Margins to the Centre*. London: Routledge, 2014.

Tsuboi, Masahito et al. "Comparative Support for the Expensive Tissue Hypothesis: Big Brains Are Correlated with Smaller Gut and Greater Parental Investment in Lake Tanganyika Cichlids." *Evolution* 69, no. 1 (2015): 190–200.

Weitzenfeld, Adam, and Melanie Joy. "An Overview of Anthropocentrism, Humanism and Specisim in Critical Animal Theory." In Nocella II et al., eds. 3–27.

White, Richard, and Erika Cudworth. "Taking It to the Streets: Challenging Systems of Domination From Below." In Nocella et al., eds. 202–219.

wild animals in the city

jenna mcfarland & andrea hunt

calgary wildlife rehabilitation society

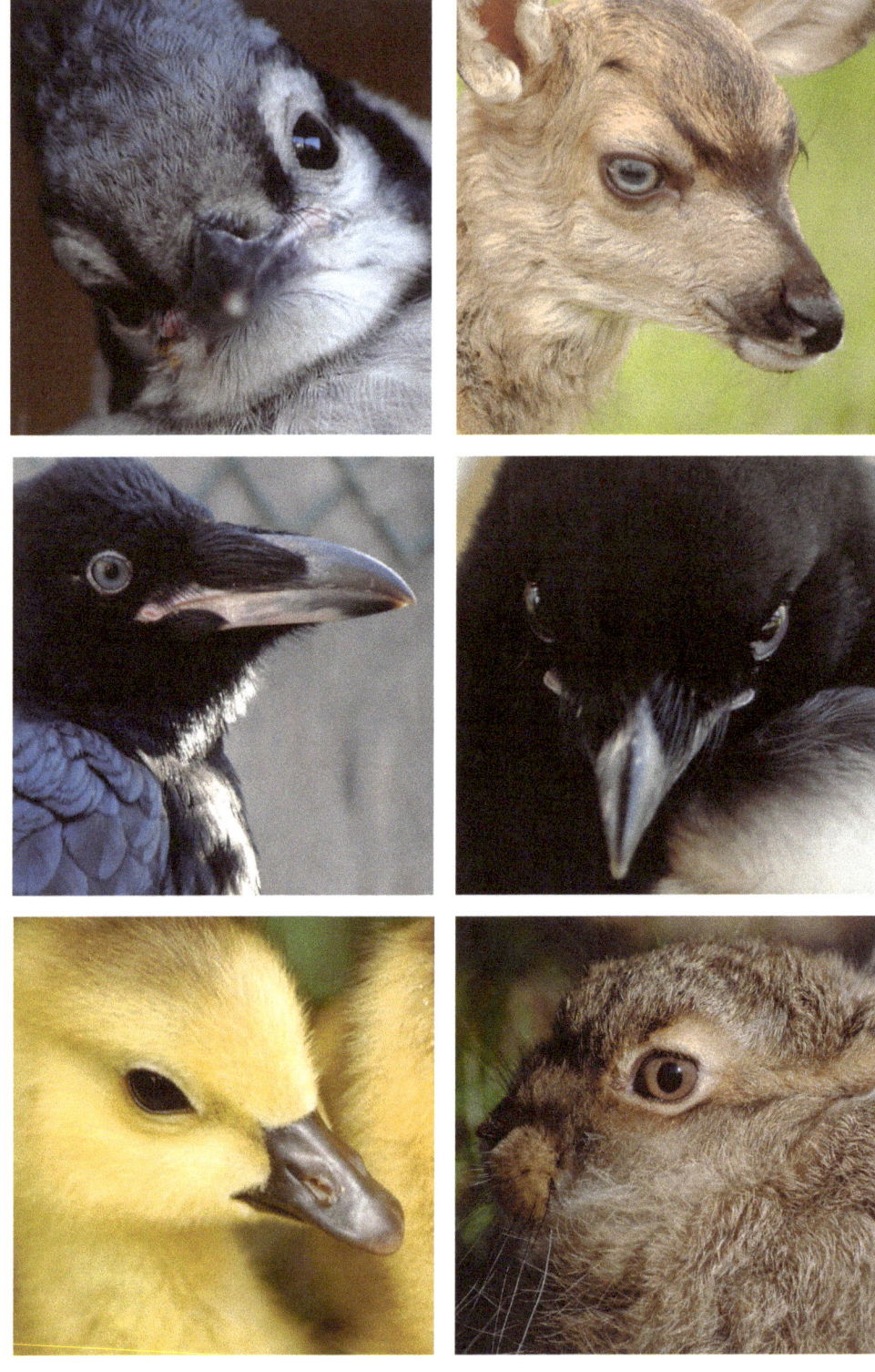

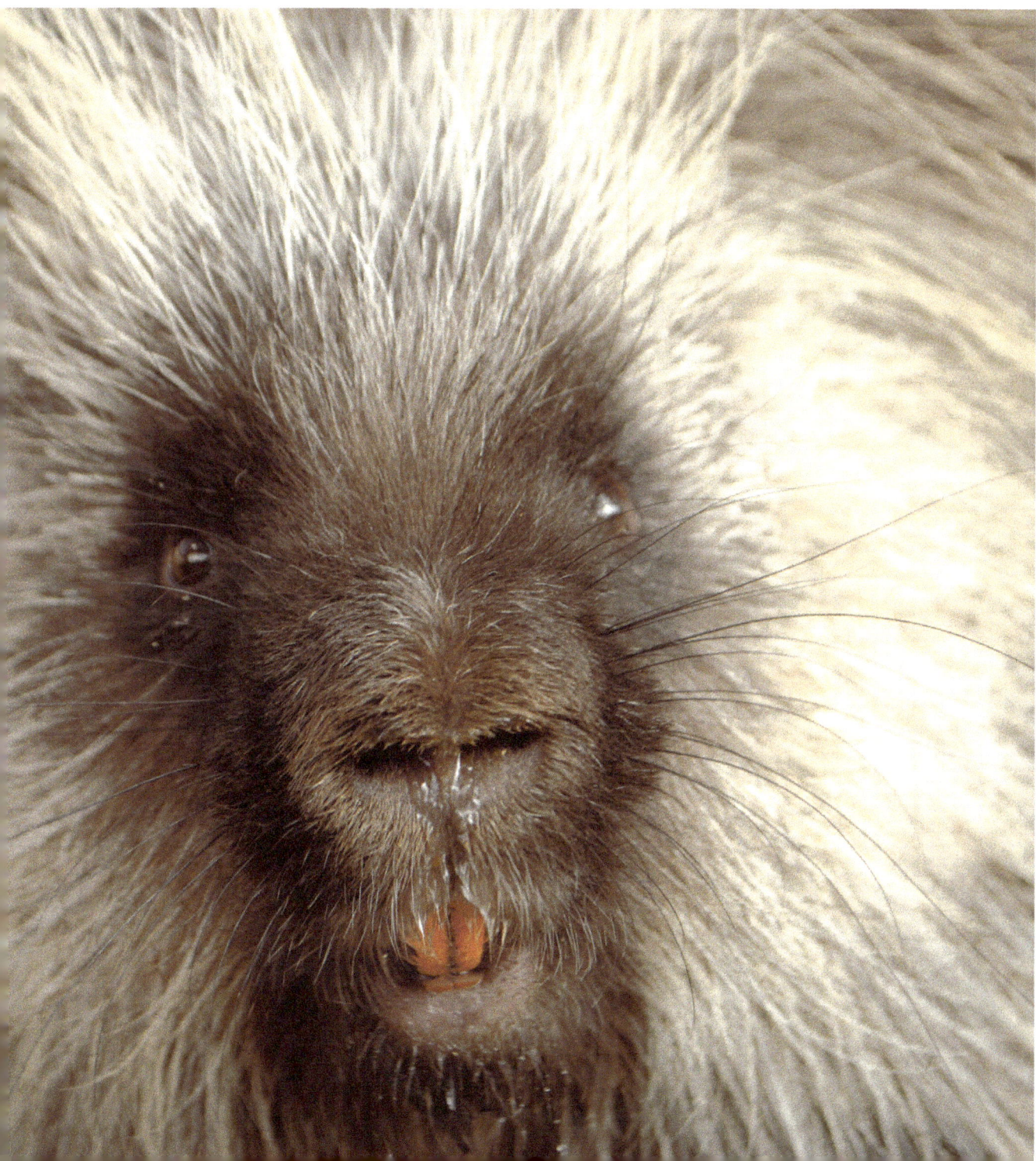

Calgary sits at the confluence of the Elbow and Bow Rivers, a corridor that supports not just the people who live here but also a rich legacy of natural abundance and biodiversity. Calgarians are proud of the city's numerous parks and open spaces as well as our connection to nature enhanced by living in such close proximity to the Rocky Mountains and the federally protected lands encased within them. The parks and wild spaces of Calgary provide habitats for over 400 species of wild animals. The lives of many citizens of Calgary are enriched daily by these flourishing wildlife populations that help to define the landscape of our city.

The Calgary Wildlife Rehabilitation Society (CWRS) has been an integral member of the Calgary community since 1993, committed to mitigating the negative impact of humans on wildlife. Our role within the community is to rehabilitate injured and orphaned wildlife, an imperative that is unique within the city limits of Calgary. The vast majority of our patients (over 2,000 per year) come to us through interactions with everyday human life. Whether they involve being caught in barbed wire, electrocuted on power lines, burned by natural gas flares, injured by striking windows, or being hit by cars, the negative impacts that humans have on urban wildlife are clear when you step into our hospital. These animals are victims of our encroachment on their native habitats and of the conflict between human activity and wild behaviours. Most of our patients are familiar species to urbanites; Canada geese, white-tailed jackrabbits, mallards, robins, magpies, and crows. We accept animals from all over southern Alberta; the range of species amazes even the most seasoned biologists among us! Shifts in migratory paths and fluctuations in climate patterns bring new and unusual species through our city (and our doors) every year.

As Calgary expands and encroaches upon spaces that were previously wild, more and more wildlife find refuge and habitat within the city limits. At CWRS we are always so surprised to hear complaints from everyday people who, having paid a premium for park-side, ravine-abutting and river-view properties, are shocked to see wildlife in their own backyards. We spend so much time answering our wildlife hotline, explaining to stunned homeowners why wild animals have chosen to "trespass" on their properties. We take the time to carefully analyze each situation and make suggestions as to how such encounters can be deterred or avoided. If we had a quarter for every time we heard, "these animals don't pay my taxes," day-to-day operations at this not-for-profit wildlife hospital would be so much easier.

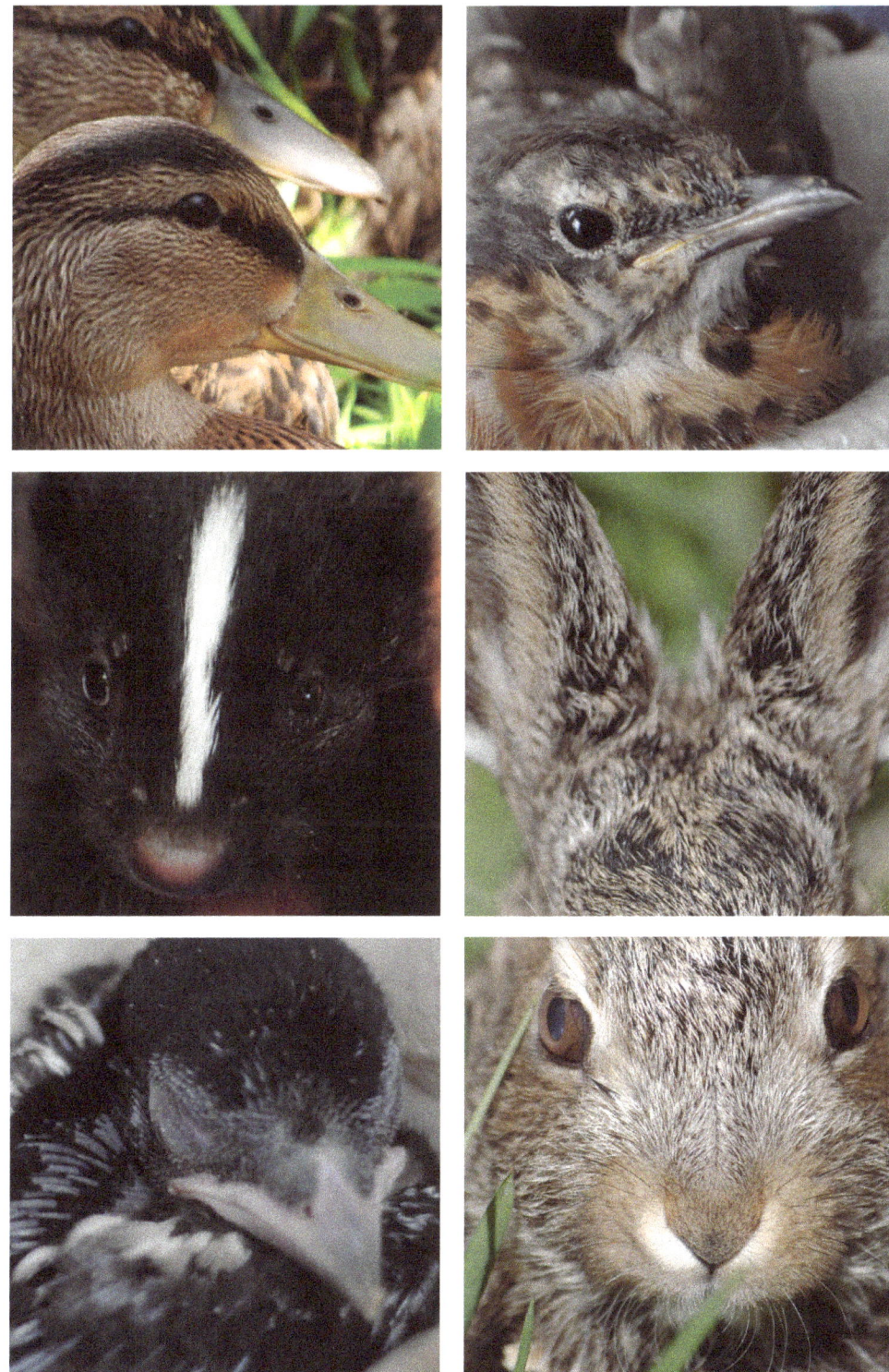

photos: Andrea S. H. Hunt. Photos courtesy of the Calgary Wildlife Rehabilitation Society

Would it not be more effective to educate ourselves on the local fauna of our region than to fight the appearance of wildlife in our backyards? To acquire, at the very least, an understanding of the behaviour and natural history of the animals that live among us? A little bit of information goes such a long way. It is startling to hear how many people think that striped skunk spray is poisonous, that North American porcupines can shoot their quills, and that jackrabbits are vectors of rabies. Day after day we reiterate that birds, with their poor sense of smell, will not reject their babies if they are touched by a bare hand, contaminated by our human odour. It seems that passing on these tall tales and myths of our youth is more popular than obtaining true knowledge.

Living with wildlife means exercising patience while enjoying the wonder of the natural cycles of wildlife: waiting a month or two for a litter of skunk kits to grow up and move out of your yard; keeping your dog on a leash while songbirds are fledging; tolerating that Canada goose's aggressive behaviour as she nests on your deck. Wildlife enriches the lives of every Calgarian, and allowing for natural behaviours is a small price to pay to have the opportunity to observe the diverse species that call our city home.

For us to co-flourish with wildlife, there first needs to be recognition of the inherent value each individual life has within the ecosystem and then we need to reframe our experiences with, and expectations of, wildlife. Even so-called nuisance species such as Richardson ground squirrels and striped skunks perform highly valuable functions within the ecosystem and need to be seen as important links within a great chain. It is for this reason that the ethics of the destruction or displacement of these animals should embrace a larger context including the niche that animal fills within the ecosystem and the consequences of its removal. Oftentimes the culling of wildlife that are considered pests has unintended negative consequences for wildlife and humans alike. Urban and rural wildlife management strategies are generally more successful when they include an analysis of the benefits of wildlife and their natural behaviours in the entire system.

As stewards of this land, it is imperative that citizens develop an appreciation for wildlife and find ways to harmoniously co-exist with the creatures that share our city. It is becoming increasingly clear that humans need wild spaces in order to maintain mental, emotional, and even physical health. Allowing for spaces that create a sense of connection to nature has to be part of a larger, more synergistic approach to managing human stress and health. Healthy ecosystems benefit every life within them, including humans. The wildlife that inhabit our city contribute to its vibrancy, its beauty, and its diverse wealth. They are worth protecting.

light pollution

in an animal city

maureen luchsinger & laura griffin

ann & sandy cross conservation area

The Ann and Sandy Cross Conservation Area (ASCCA) is a 4,800-acre day-use natural area that was originally a ranch owned by Sandy Cross. Sandy understood that the well-being of the abundance of wildlife that shared his home was dependent on the landscape. Landscape is an important part of a healthy ecosystem. Upon retirement, Sandy and his wife Ann, being aware of the ongoing growth of neighbouring Calgary, decided to preserve the natural habitat of the ranch for future generations. They were able to do this by donating their land as a conservation area for the protection of native wildlife habitat. To this day the ASCCA continues to provide space for native species of wildlife and to offer conservation education programs that do not jeopardize wildlife and habitat.

The ASCCA recognizes there are natural ecosystems throughout any urban environment, which require stewardship from their human inhabitants in order to co-flourish with the wildlife. The urban ecology of Calgary is facing significant changes in the landscape, including the degradation of parts of the natural world. In order to co-exist within the urban ecology with our non-human animals, we need to demonstrate that the natural environment is an important and critical aspect of our lives, by making decisions that value its health and longevity. Being able to make informed decisions requires environmental education to ensure people regard nature as part of the world they live in and not separate from it.

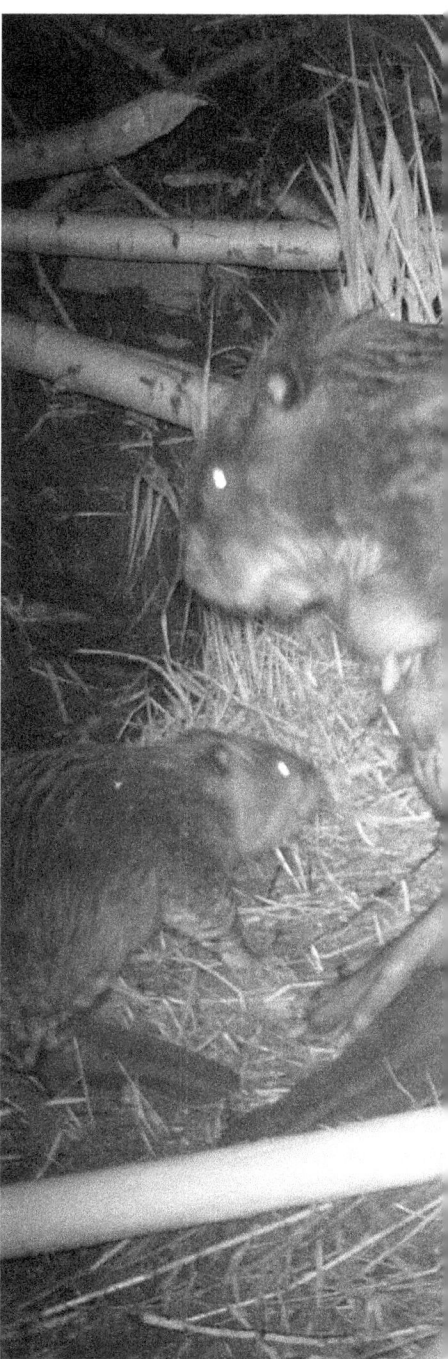

One significant change to Calgary's urban ecology is increased light pollution. Ensuring dark spaces occur for a specific interval of time is essential to everyone's overall well-being. Humans can alter their lifeways in order to mitigate these problems, but as Calgary continues to expand it must embrace the darkness of the urban landscape and mitigate light pollution so that non-human animals and humans can co-flourish.

Light pollution refers to any artificial light that illuminates the nocturnal sky and has a disruptive effect on natural cycles and inhibits our view of celestial objects. Although humans have been introducing light into the nighttime environment since they first started playing with fire, light pollution is a relatively new environmental concern. With current technology, humans are now capable of essentially extending the day to suit their pleasure—a luxury that science is now discovering comes with a price. We need to slow down and reflect on the impacts of our choices within the entire ecosystem.

Light at night impacts several aspects of animal behaviour: it changes foraging patterns due to light attraction or avoidance, reduces the ability of some species to find mates, inhibits the ability of birds, insects, animals, and humans to navigate using the stars, and interferes with the natural circadian rhythms—the 24-hour day and night cycle that controls an organism's biological clock through hormone regulation. In animals (including humans) and plants, melatonin is the hormone which regulates the ebb and flow of other hormones in the body. In turn, these other hormones repair damaged tissues, fight infections, and perform several other important tasks in the body. Studies have shown melatonin production is significantly decreased without prolonged periods of dark. When days are extended with artificial lighting an organism's ability to function in a healthy way is thus significantly inhibited.

Simple steps can be taken to reduce light pollution and regain some of the health of urban ecology. Light fixtures can be shielded to prevent wasted and sometimes hazardous light. Light bulbs can be changed to low-wattage, energy-efficient bulbs. One of the simplest methods of taking back the dark of the night is for humans to choose

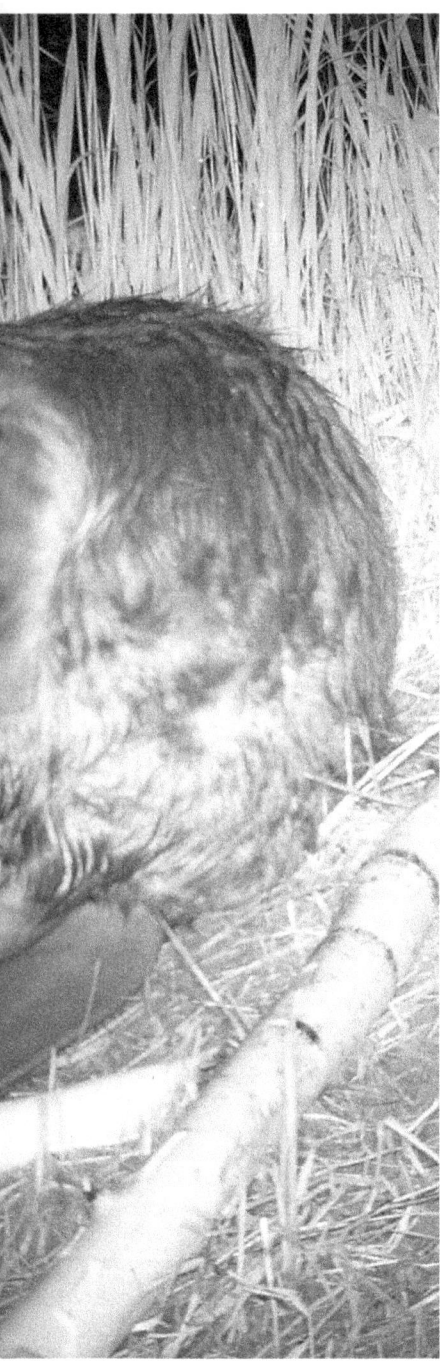

to turn off lights when they are not being used. Preventing light pollution in Calgary is a plausible means to help the animals within it co-flourish as healthy members of a biodiverse community. There is growing international recognition of the importance of natural and urban areas with little or no light pollution. Pristine dark natural areas are helpful in understanding the quality of the ecosystem and the biodiversity within. Understanding and exploring these interactions with nature ties into biophilia, the innate emotional need humans have for contact with other living beings. These experiences will provide connections humans need to build a deeper understanding of themselves and the world around them, and encourage them to recognize that they are one of many organisms in an ecosystem.

For thousands of years humans have been able to look up at night and see stars, the Milky Way, and the giant expanse of the universe. Their knowledge and wisdom was attained through their interconnectedness with all aspects of the environment, both physical and spiritual. This has contributed to several advances throughout the Anthropocene, the discovery that the earth was not the centre of the universe being one of the most humbling and controversial, as it introduced the thought that humans were but a small part of an immense mosaic. Would it not be of benefit if urban animals could once again see the stars and experience this connection? Returning the darkness of night to the urban landscapes is a small stewardship step to help humans co-flourish with the biodiversity that remains within the city—a step that has the potential to shed a new light on humanity.

ASCCA was designated as Canada's first Nocturnal Preserve in 2015 by the Royal Astronomical Society of Canada. We recognize the importance of Dark Sky Preserves, Urban Star Parks, Nocturnal Preserves, and International Dark Sky designations as an integral part of ecosystem health.

excerpt from # our bio

our vision [52]

Calgarians value our city's diversity and richness in wildlife, vegetation and landscapes; The City of Calgary and citizens work to integrate our actions and the built environment with an ecological network that is healthy, connected and well managed.

our principles

As natural systems are dynamic, we recognize the indefinite time horizon for achieving biodiversity conservation in Calgary. A principled approach—rather than a goal-based approach—enables us to be dynamic in our actions as we move towards our vision. We have established four central principles to guide our decision-making. They act as a foundation for our behaviours and actions towards biodiversity conservation.

Ecological literacy: The City of Calgary supports the conservation and appreciation of biodiversity by cultivating knowledge and understanding about ecological processes, personal stewardship actions and Calgary's natural heritage.

Ecological resilience: The City of Calgary plans, protects, manages and restores open space in Calgary for productive, diverse, healthy ecosystems with the capacity to recover from disturbance and adapt to change.

Collaboration: The City of Calgary works jointly and shares responsibility with individuals and groups to advance biodiversity and ecological resilience locally, regionally and globally.

Integration: The City of Calgary works with communities and businesses to build neighbourhoods that support local biodiversity conservation, healthy ecological processes and provide equitable access to nature.

divercity

calgary's 10-year biodiversity strategic plan

our commitments

Our commitments outline how we are dedicated to supporting our vision of biodiversity.

ecological literacy

a) Develop volunteer initiatives and education programs to support environmental stewardship and biodiversity conservation in collaboration with schools, communities and citizens.

b) Ensure appropriate City of Calgary staff, Council, businesses and communities have access to training and information to advance the goals of biodiversity conservation, through procurement practices; building and site design; open space planning and management, as well as awareness of invasive species, habitat fragmentation and loss, indirect pressures on biodiversity and how they disrupt ecological processes.

c) Set objectives and targets for biodiversity conservation across appropriate literacy initiatives.

d) Make biodiversity conservation a common element in municipal decision-making.

ecological resilience

a) Monitor the city's natural areas and water bodies to develop an approach that ensures they are more resilient to disturbance while retaining healthy function, structure, feedback loops and integrity.

b) Retain, acquire and maintain large contiguous or connected natural areas, with supportive built environments, providing connections with the greater region.

c) Reduce direct pressures on biodiversity through managing appropriate access and use in areas rich in biodiversity and natural heritage.

d) Reduce invasive species through identifying threats, implementing measures to prevent their establishment while monitoring and controlling these species where necessary.

e) Conserve habitat function by supporting native and non-invasive locally adapted species.

f) Maintain significant ecological processes such as fire and flood in appropriate natural areas.

collaboration

a) Recognize the financial, social and environmental cost of removing or modifying natural systems in developing Calgary and include consideration of these costs in municipal decision-making.

b) Recognize biodiversity and healthy natural systems as an aspect of good economic development in Calgary.

c) Partner with researchers, government and institutions to advance research and innovation in biodiversity conservation.

d) Remove knowledge and institutional barriers to protecting biodiversity.

integration

a) Increase habitat diversity in private, public and institutional open space to support ecologically healthy neighbourhoods and aid appropriate access to and use of nature for citizens.

b) Develop a database that integrates land use and biodiversity data to support strategic management of Calgary's ecosystems.

c) Plan and manage Calgary parks and open space as a connected network of habitats and wildlife movement corridors, with the aim of reducing roadway collision threats and related human–urban wildlife conflict.

d) Develop infrastructure that mimics and incorporates ecological processes.

e) Manage open space to positively respond to both sudden and gradual environmental changes, such as extreme weather events and climate change.

f) Preserve rare landscape features and critical habitats within and between neighbourhoods.

our procedures

Meeting our commitments will require specific actions. We have established four procedures, each with multiple initiatives in support of the procedure. With the launch of each project, the City will develop roles and responsibilities, budgets, stakeholder engagement plans and specific performance measures to ensure and monitor successful execution.

procedure 1
foster ecological literacy

Increase public understanding of biodiversity and ecological processes to encourage positive actions that support environmental conservation.

The following are possible practices and projects that would support the procedure:

a) Deliver a city-wide ecological literacy program.

b) Work with key partners to promote community engagement with broader ecological stewardship initiatives, such as building pollinator-friendly and biologically diverse community gardens, developing wildlife habitat conservation initiatives and establishing neighbourhood greening programs.

c) Develop and implement a framework to integrate knowledge of Calgary's natural heritage into conservation and education opportunities.

d) Develop and implement a strategy to inspire citizens to take positive stewardship actions through volunteer, school, corporate and community environmental education programs and initiatives.

e) Provide a range of programs and tools that encourage Calgarians to engage with biodiversity in the city's built and natural environments.

f) Continue the biodiversity oral history project to showcase Calgarians' personal connections to biodiversity.

g) Establish an artist-in-residence program to advance biodiversity literacy.

procedure 2
improve the city of calgary's ecological functions

Restore degraded habitats and manage biodiversity to increase the overall health, function and resilience of Calgary's open space and neighbourhoods.

The following are possible practices and projects that would support the procedure:

a) Implementing habitat restoration projects in critical areas for local ecosystem function, structure, quality and resilience.

b) Develop and implement management plans for all status species in Calgary parks and open space.

c) Restore underused manicured park space to increase plant diversity and habitat complexity and function.

d) Encourage the restoration of private, community, business and institutional lands.

e) Develop and implement landscaping design guidelines to establish appropriate soil fertility, volume and management that support the land use goals of new or redeveloped open space.

f) Develop and implement a list of preferred planting species for developers and The City of Calgary.

g) Implement strategies to reduce invasive species and their spread in Calgary.

h) Develop and implement alternative open space management practices including grazing, prescribed burns and restoration, as well as educational messages and opportunities for public understanding.

procedure 3

instill biodiversity values across the city of calgary

Collaborate to establish conservation values and practices into planning, managing and operating The City of Calgary and living in Calgary neighbourhoods.

The following are possible practices and projects that would support the procedure:

a) Encourage champions within The City of Calgary to help ensure biodiversity principles are adhered to throughout City planning, managing and implementing initiatives.

b) Develop and implement a biodiversity communications strategy.

c) Initiate a biodiversity steering committee with representatives from The City, Council, local businesses, environmental non-governmental organizations, academia and citizens at large to advance the commitments of *Our BiodiverCity*.

d) Continue to identify and align with other City plans, strategies and programs that have biodiversity-related components.

e) Develop and implement a biodiversity project recognition program for community, private business and City projects.

f) Ensure biodiversity goals are captured in appropriate city planning frameworks, for example the *Corporate Project Management Framework*.

g) Develop policies and guidelines to ensure people are allowed equitable access to areas of biodiversity.

procedure 4

integrate with wildlife, plants and natural heritage

Conserve lands and waters that are critical in retaining essential local ecosystem function, structure, quality and resilience, while ensuring appropriate access and use.

The following are possible practices and projects that would support the procedure:

a) Develop and implement an assessment of existing Calgary parks that would aid in setting conservation priorities and monitoring health to create and sustain functional habitat.

b) Develop and implement policies and guidelines to conserve and connect ecological cores and corridors through a city-wide review of existing and proposed open space. These may include design requirements of green roofs and living walls; protection of ecological cores and corridors; design of wildlife crossings for urban barriers; park design; regulation of topsoil conservation; salvage/relocation of vegetation and habitats; bylaws; and design development guidelines.

c) Map and implement a framework to acquire lands of high ecological and cultural value that can't be otherwise protected through the subdivision process.

d) Establish data-sharing agreements and strategic collaborations with government, industry, research organizations, other municipalities and the public.

e) Develop and implement a municipal wildlife management strategy.

f) Work collaboratively with neighbouring and regional municipalities to identify opportunities to increase biodiversity across the region.

g) Develop and implement an incentive program to promote the use of ecological easements.

measuring success:
3 biodiversity targets

Under the section "Pressures on biodiversity," we noted three common challenges in cities that directly affect biodiversity conservation and ecological processes: habitat fragmentation, habitat loss and invasive species. We've developed three broad-scale targets to monitor these pressures and therefore to measure the successful trajectory of our strategic plan.

By 2025, we will address three pressures on biodiversity in the following ways:

habitat fragmentation

Evaluate landscapes in Calgary and set targets for conservation measures to identify, protect and manage ecological cores and corridors.

habitat loss

Restore 20 per cent of Calgary's current open space to support the conservation of biodiversity.

invasive species

Identify invasive species in Calgary's open space and complete strategies for their management.

One Yellow Rabbit ensemble

squirrel 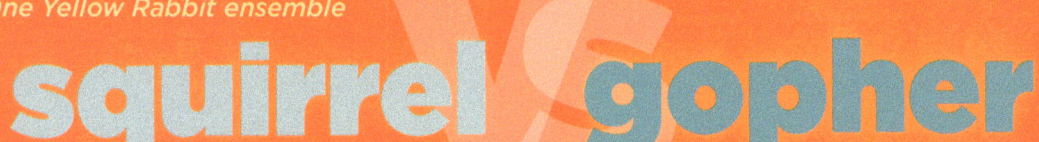 gopher

from calgary i love you but you're killing me

calgary i love you . . . premiered at the 30th High Performance Rodeo in 2016.
The production featured Denise Clarke (Magpie), Andy Curtis (Squirrel),
Karen Hines (Gopher), & Jamie Tognazzini.

squirrel: Their tails are small and jumpy
In trees you'll find them not
Gophers sleep beneath the ground
Disgusted by all nuts
They turn away from nuts

I have some pretty gopher friends
We hang, I like them lots
I don't invite them to my house
They are mystified by nuts

gopher: I'm turned off by his nuts

gopher: Squirrels climb those tall trees
They chitter never peep
They'd rather climb a dirty pole
Than roll around in weeds
I love to roll in weeds

There are squirrels at my gym
They clean up really nice
I cannot bring them to my place
They don't like dandelions

squirrel: Repelled by dandelions

gopher: They don't like dandelions

full cast: Some of them are my friends
But I'd rather breed with a mitten
What would my family say
If brought one home for Christmas?

magpie: I wheel and turn above you
A corvid optimist
I get along with everyone
If I keep my distance
If I keep my distance

I'll eat nuts and dandelions
And when the cars accrue
I'll sit upon a fence and wait
For sandwiches of you
And pancakes made of you!

gopher: Of me?

magpie: Of you!

squirrel: Of me?

magpie: Of you!

gopher & squirrel: Oh no!

magpie: Of YOU!

musical break

full cast: Some of them are my friends but
I'd rather breed with a mitten
What would my family say
If brought one out to the cabin?

gopher: My mother would make you sleep in a pup tent.

magpie: I like pup tents.

gopher: Excuse me you guys, I just have to go across the road.

squirrel: **Watch out for that car!**

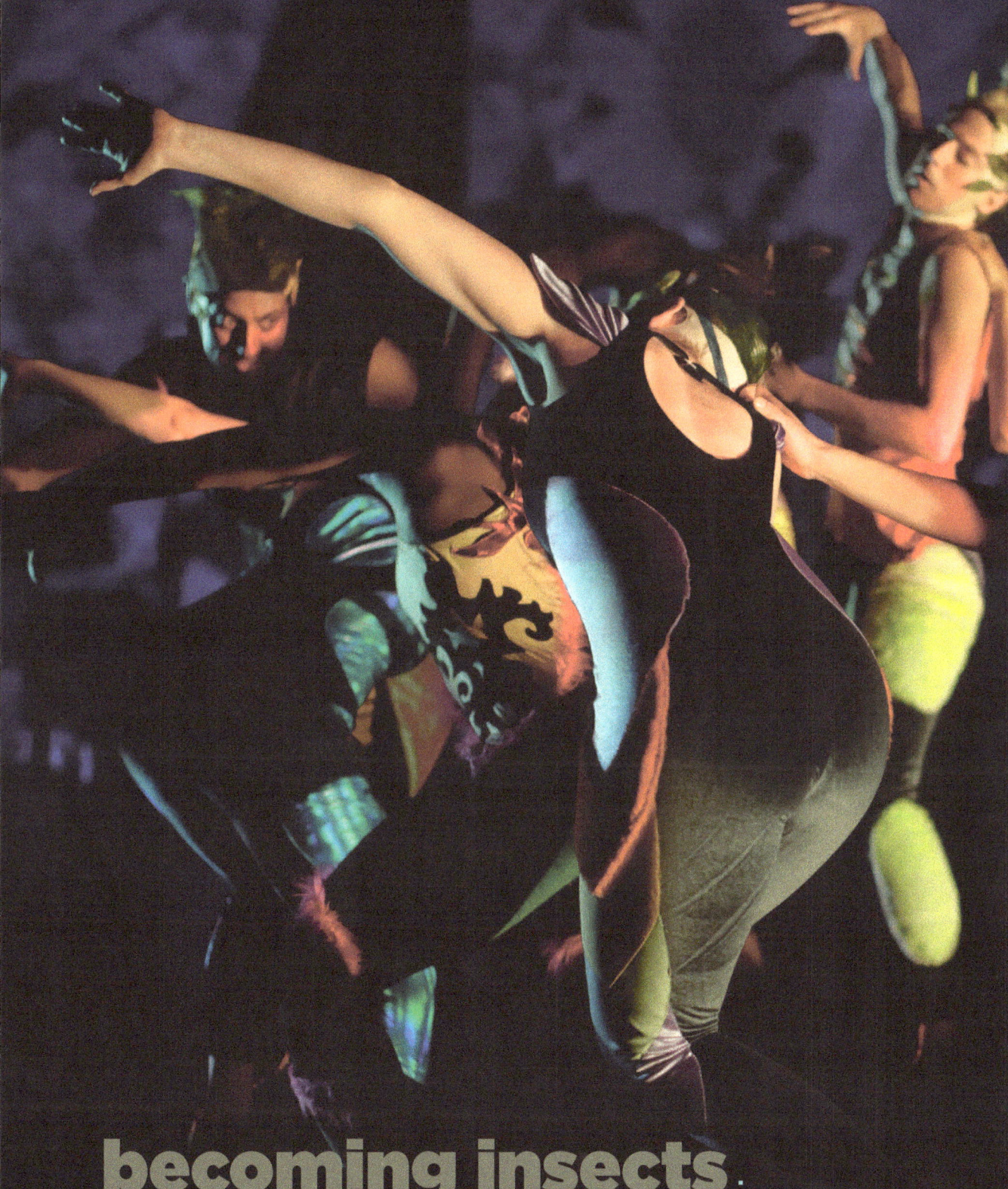

becoming insects a new universe

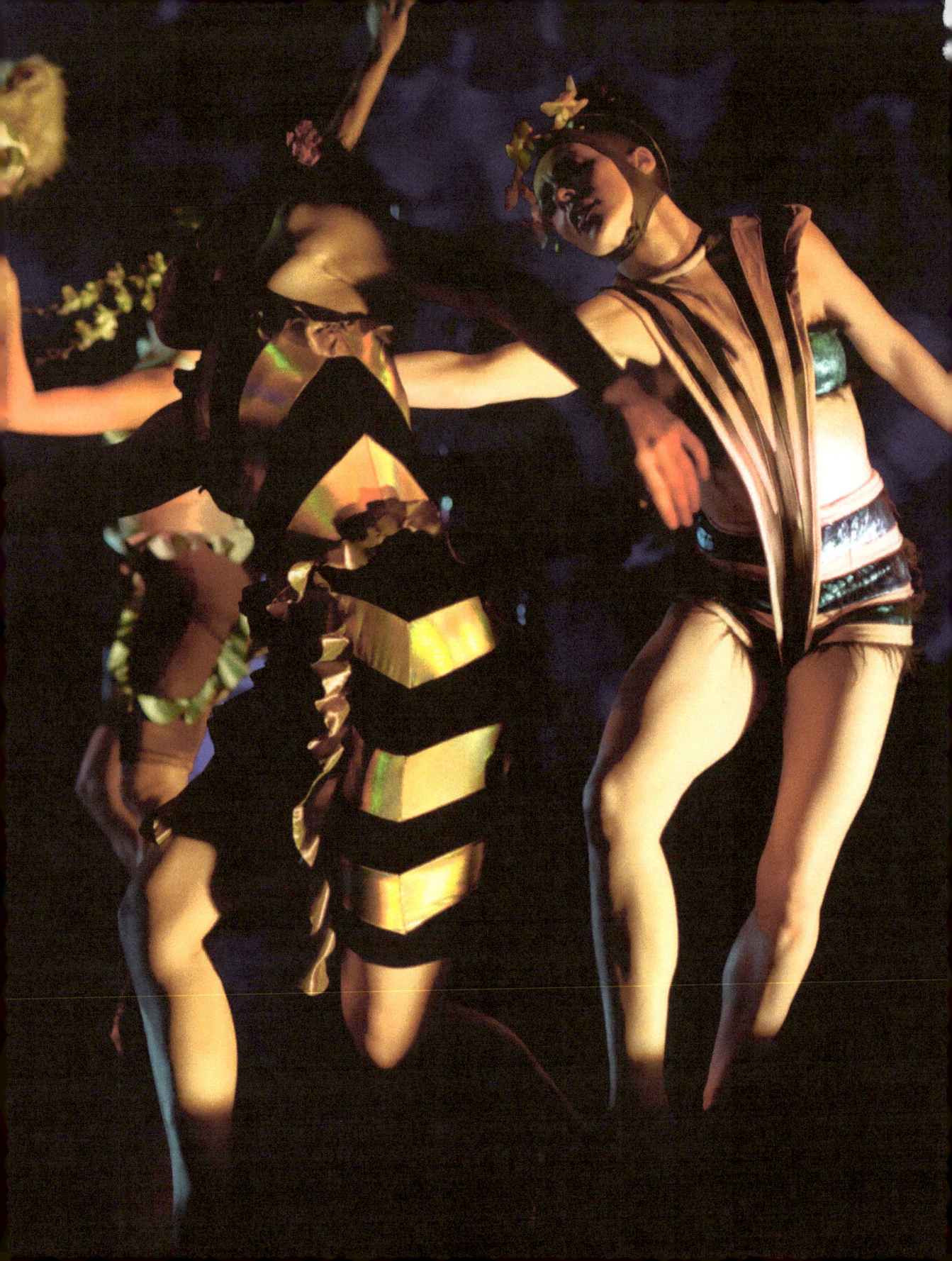

kimberley cooper
decidedly jazz dance works

Jazz was born in North America of African and European parents as a result of the slave trade. In Africa, all aspects of life were celebrated and ritualized through dance and music, including farming and hunting. We can see how the frequent animal mimicry in these rituals eventually evolved into early twentieth-century African-American social jazz dances such as the Turkey Trot, Bunny Hug, Buzzard Lope, and Grizzly Bear.

Maybe it's the African parent of jazz that inspires me to create movement that has an animal or creature-esque source. Maybe it's my insatiable curiosity about movement, keeping my eyes open to the world of 2, 4, 6, 100-legged creatures, that drives me to explore different ways of approaching gravity, the spine, and relationships. Creatures inspire a distinctive approach to emotion in performance, and tapping into instinct, rather than emotion, can sometimes inspire a more compelling performance.

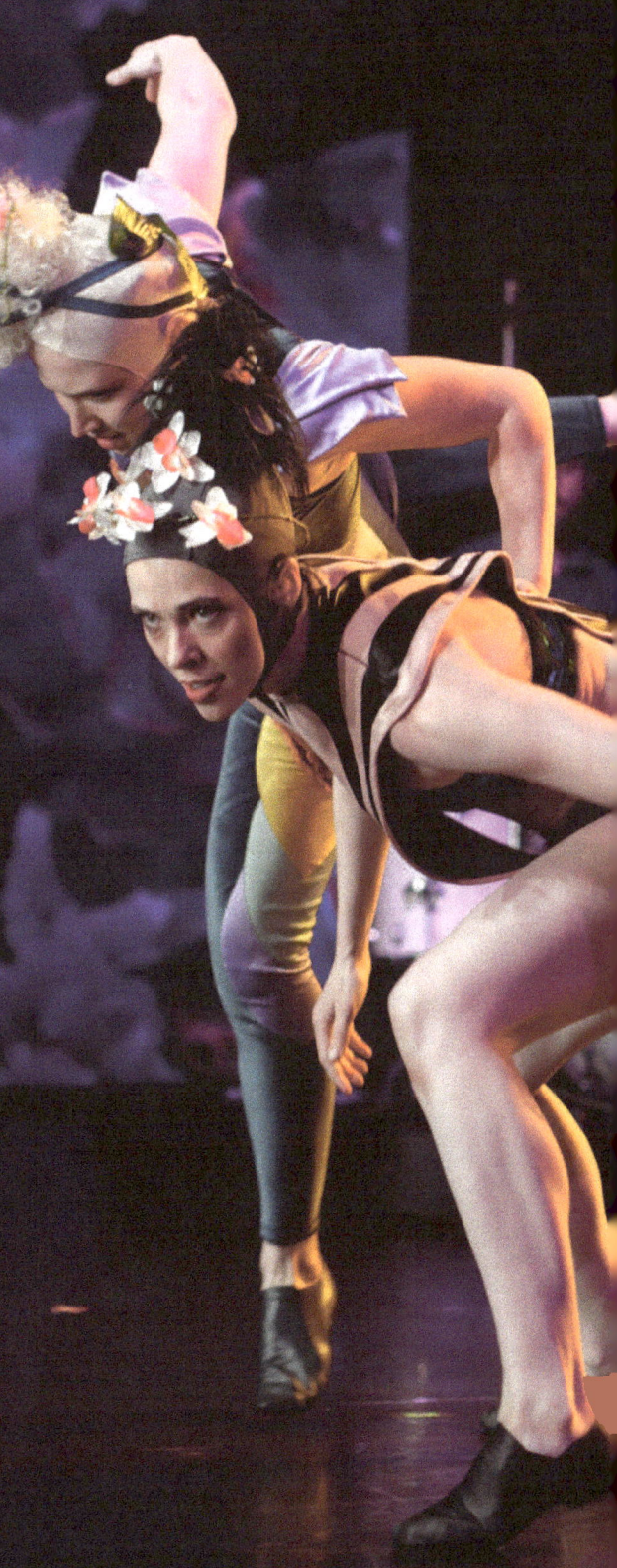

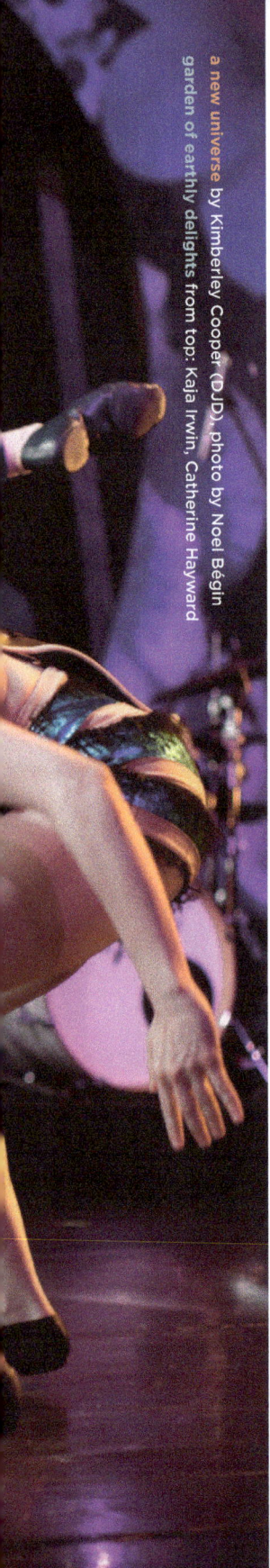

a new universe by Kimberley Cooper (DJD), photo by Noel Bégin
garden of earthly delights from top: Kaja Irwin, Catherine Hayward

I never liked bugs, but they seemed to like me. I get five mosquito bites for every one of yours. My mother always said we had sweet blood. Spiders, ants, roaches—when I'm somewhere they are, they always come to, well, bug me. Then I met a praying mantis.

It was the most beautiful bug I'd ever seen. It was night, in a small town in northeastern Brazil in 2013. It flew like a fairy and it fascinated me, so much so that I wanted to touch it, which I never want to do. It let me pet its back and it hung around for a long time, posing for photos, eating other bugs. It changed things for me. I began to imagine the universe it lived in.

Then I started looking at more bugs. I watched countless films and videos, including *Microcosmos*, the 1996 documentary showing the lives of insects in a field in France. Seeds were planted with its images. I watched bugs and other creatures in my own backyard, squirmy worms that magically seemed to move, spiders with their amazing strength, dragonflies with their wild flight patterns. I became fascinated with all of these little worlds, these communities of anthills and spiders' nests, that we humans often barely notice.

This research led to *New Universe*, a piece I created in 2016. The movement was highly informed by insects. It was part nature show, part comment on society, part Hieronymus Bosch painting. There were five sections in the piece, each with its own flavour. There was a sense of evolution and expansion throughout, starting in a condensed claustrophobic setting. As the piece progressed, everything, including the space and the dancers, became more open and naked.

Though the movement was inspired by insects, *New Universe* was often quite human. At times the dancers were insectile with human characteristics, at times they were the reverse. For example, the piece began with a woman finding a giant piece of bubblegum, chewing it, and becoming high from the sugar. As this section continued and more dancers were introduced, the scene became a madhouse of scrambling and fighting for sugar, exactly what happens if you drop something sweet beside an anthill, which in fact I did as part of my research (although in our version the dancers erupted into the jitterbug). Through one lens it was quite comical, watching these greedy, cockroach-inspired characters fighting and responding to the sugar rush; through another, one could see addicts fighting to get high.

previous image
a new universe by Kimberley Cooper (DJD), photo by Noel Bégin
caterpillar, from left: Kaleb Tekeste, Natasha Korney, Audrey Gaussiran, Shayne Johnson, Sabrina Comanescu, Julia Cosentino, Catherine Hayward

The creative process is always an adventure; for me, there is no formula to art making. In my practice, I spend a lot of time in the studio, dancing and generating movement that feels and looks a certain way. The different parts of this piece came together in a variety of ways. For example, there was a section in the piece that we referred to in the studio as "rhythm bugs." The process for creating the movement went like this:

I chose a piece of music. The music was being written (and played live) by William Parker, a composer and bassist from New York. It's often tricky to be creating a dance piece with original music that is being composed at the same time in another city, especially when, as in my work, the two are so deeply connected. Often I will use found music (recordings that exist already) as source material to have something to work with in the studio until we have the band with us, which is usually much closer to the opening of the piece because working with live music is expensive. For *New Universe*, the majority of the music was composed specifically for the piece, but some of it was re-arrangements of various pieces from William's huge collection of recordings.

After I chose the music for "rhythm bugs," I learned the drum pattern of the first couple of minutes and started making movement based on the rhythm. I was interested in using West African-inspired movement and making the music of the drum pattern come through with my feet on the floor. Instead of using traditional West African posture (quite bent at the waist, wider than hip-width legs), I narrowed my base and stood up taller, lifted my chest to the ceiling, took my gaze down my nose, shrunk my arms in,

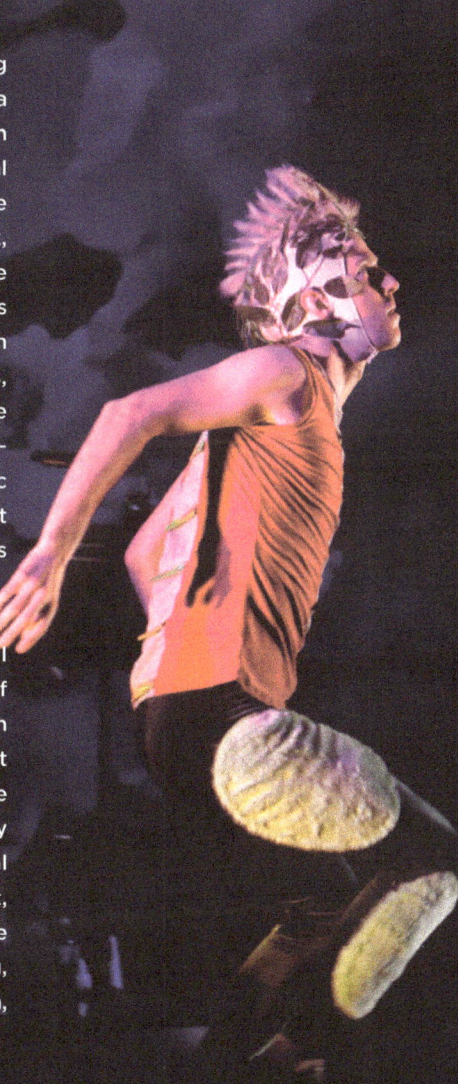

wing-like, and accentuated my wrists as I made my arms move forward and back with the movement. A kind of haughty, self-important character started to emerge. This eventually developed into the marching-off-to-war dance, with the dancers representing army ants. When we learn movement sequences that are very musical, it's easier to learn the "music" of the dance, rather than trying to count it out, so the dancers are singing the rhythm in their heads while they dance the dance. Of course the drummer didn't learn the rhythm, he improvised based on the feel, so the dancers became another instrument and added another layer of rhythm.

Another dance we called "caterpillar": there were nine dancers, each a segment of the caterpillar. They snaked around the stage and eventually the body split in two and the head and tail of the caterpillar danced a mating duet, part of which was manipulated and echoed by the other dancers. This was inspired not only by watching caterpillars move but also by watching slugs mate. They circle around and around and almost become one animal.

These are just two examples from *New Universe*. I took inspiration from cockroaches, dung beetles, scorpions, spiders, dragonflies, caterpillars, moths, butterflies, ants, wasps, stick insects, flies, and, of course, the praying mantis.

Now when I see insects I view them differently. I respect them and I actually feel that I owe them something. The creeps they used to give me have pretty much disappeared. As clichéd as it might seem, if you really take time to learn about something you can learn to appreciate it, empathize with it, and admire its beauty. I'm sure there are some bugs that I will always prefer to only see on film, but there are so many incredible creatures out there, it was lovely to be inspired by them.

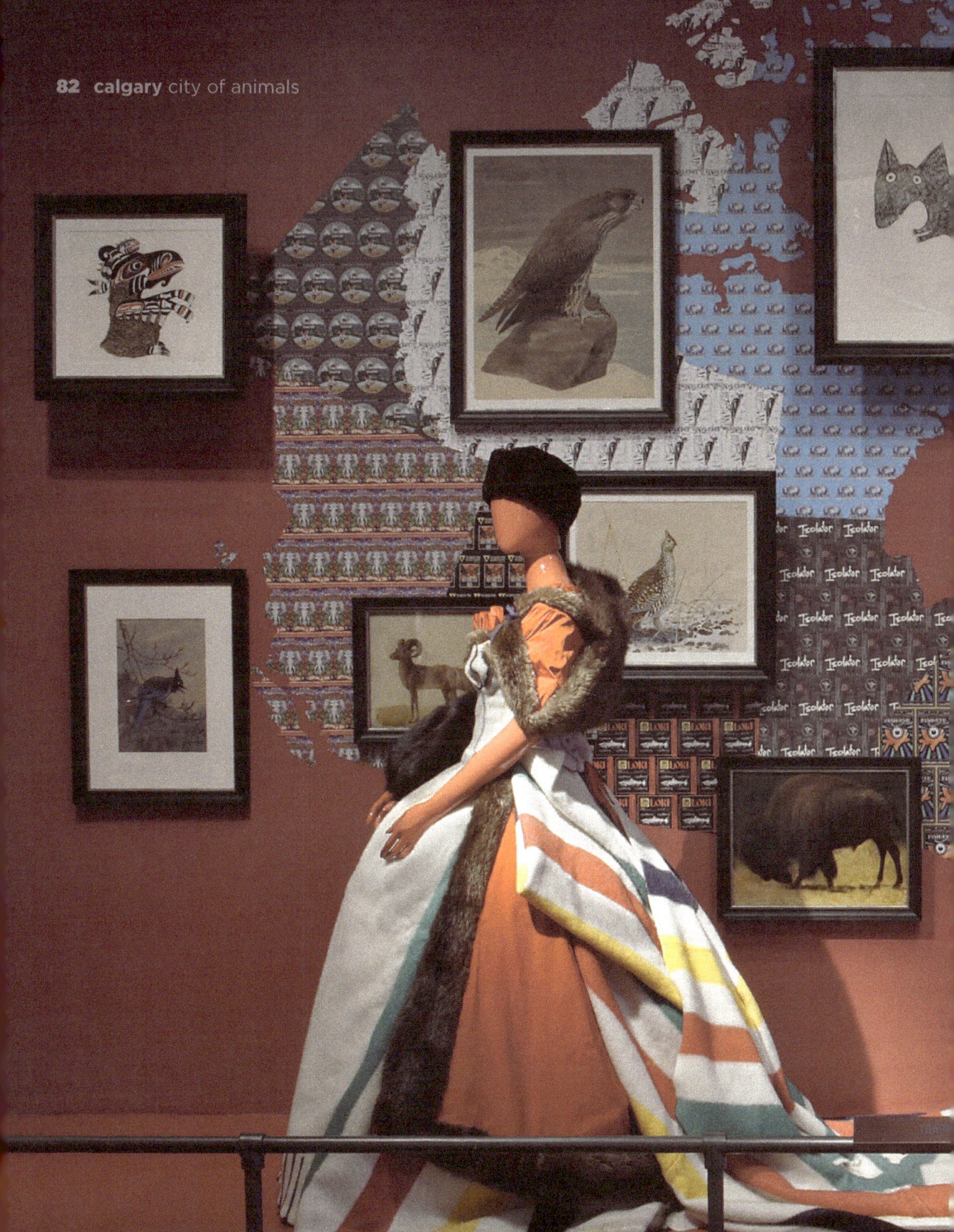

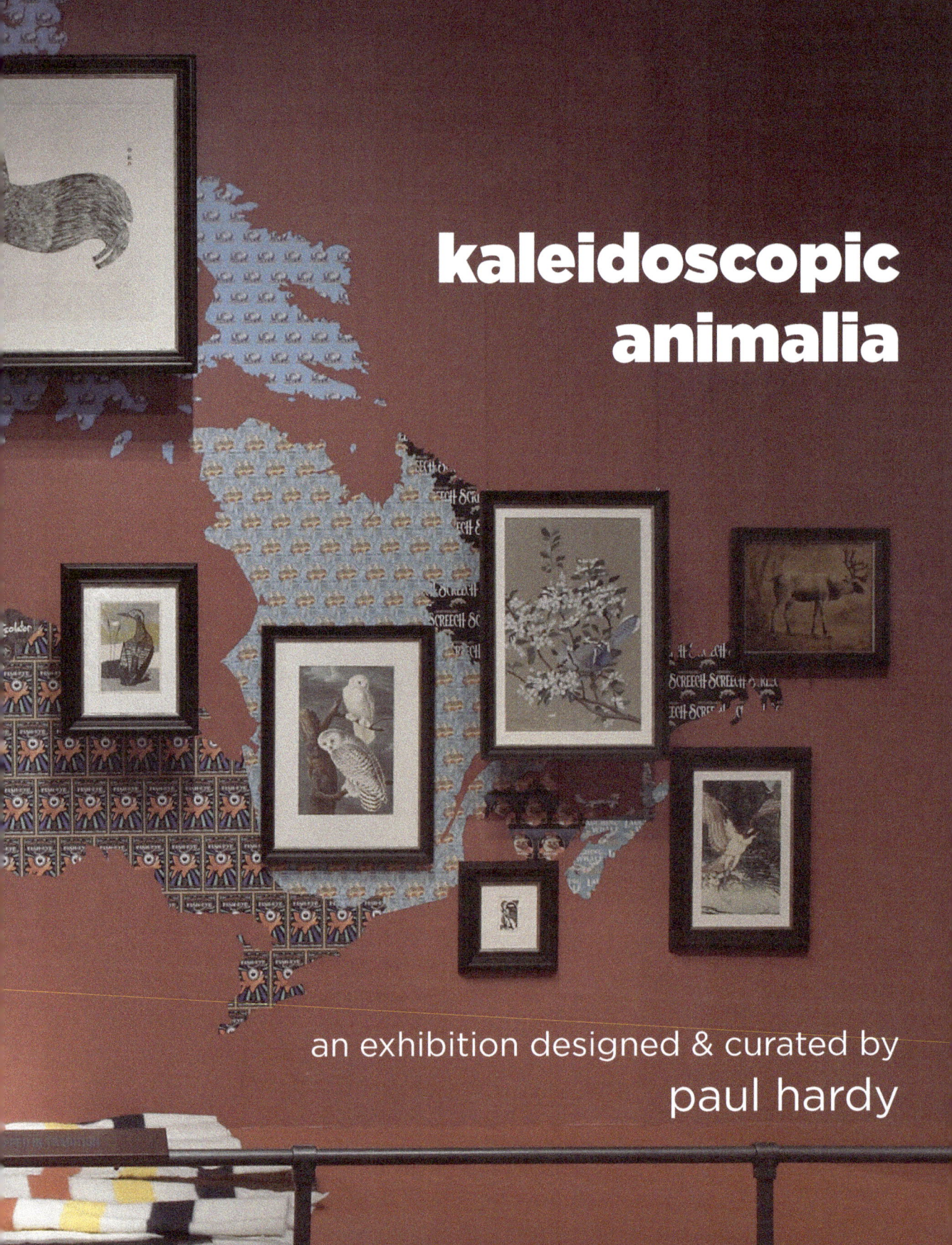

kaleidoscopic animalia

an exhibition designed & curated by
paul hardy

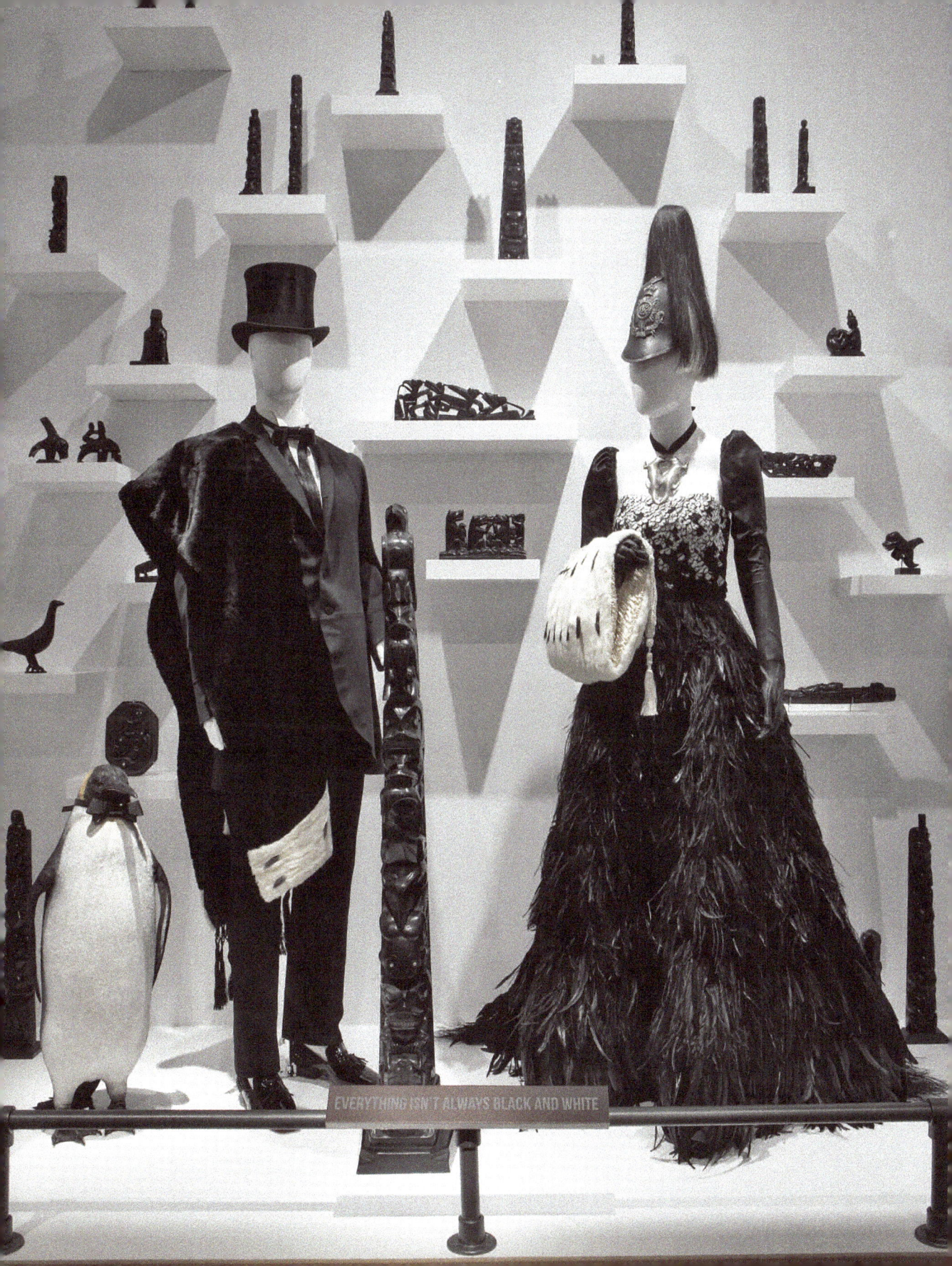

EVERYTHING ISN'T ALWAYS BLACK AND WHITE

As Glenbow's artist in residence for 2015, acclaimed Calgary-based fashion designer Paul Hardy was inspired by Glenbow's vast collection to curate an exhibition focusing on how animal imagery and symbolism have influenced human creativity across time and cultures.

Animal-inspired artifacts and artwork from every area of the museum's collection were juxtaposed with iconic fashion items and original designs Paul created for the exhibition. In fifteen thematic "windows," meant to resemble the incredible storefront windows of some of the world's most iconic department stores, Paul purposefully mixed items from different cultures as a way to highlight the universal appeal of animals, illustrate the significance of animals to many different cultures, or emphasize the timeless desire—whether functional, fashionable, or both—for animal-inspired products.

The subject of this exhibition was also an opportunity to reflect on societal views toward the use of animals for things such as fashion, and how those views have changed through time. As with many museums, Glenbow's collection contains historical objects made from now-endangered species, or materials no longer considered acceptable for use, regardless of purpose. In displaying these historical artifacts, our aim was to encourage thought and discussion about the history associated with those items, changes in values, and how we see our place in the world relative to other species, prompting conversations about consumption, conservation, creation, inspiration, art, and design.

melanie kjorlien
vp access, collections and exhibitions, glenbow

previous
trapped in tradition   Canadians' relationship with animals is ingrained in our history. This window is a unique portrayal of these deep-rooted connections, referencing the fur trade and the importance of the beaver; the influence of animals in our provincial and territorial identities; and how animal imagery is used to brand products we consume every day.

opposite
everything isn't always black and white   One of the primary inspirations for this window was Glenbow's collection of Haida argillite carvings. The carvings include images of animals, birds, fish and supernatural beings contained in stories, legends and myths that were passed down through generations and embodied in crests, designs and decoration.

Our bond with animals has existed in several forms: from a primeval interplay of hunter versus prey; to an evolution with fibers, textiles, and tanning; to utilitarian needs for farming and transport; to a union in sports, entertainment, and the domestication of pets; and to a visual appreciation of animal aesthetics as seen in arts and interiors.

Regardless of the reason, it is evident that this alliance has permeated every facet of the landscape of life—design in particular. In view of this subject's transcendent impact in global society, as Glenbow's artist in residence, I opted to gleefully examine the historic influence animals have had on design and culture, with highlights reflecting the multiculturalism of Canadian life.

My desire in creating this exhibition was to startle the viewer by creating a collision with tradition, and by presenting a fresh outlook on how we view this influence in art, interiors, lifestyle, music, and pop culture.

paul hardy

beastly fetish   This window contains an exquisite collection of accessories comprised of materials sourced from various animals or adorned with animal imagery. There are hats made of wool, hats adorned with feathers and hats decorated with stylized ravens. There are bags made of leather, satin, satin velvet and buffalo hide, and purses embellished with tortoiseshell or ivory handles. There are boots made of fur, leather, felt, satin—even a pair of foot armour decorated with animals—and shoes inlaid with mother-of-pearl.

BEASTLY FETISH

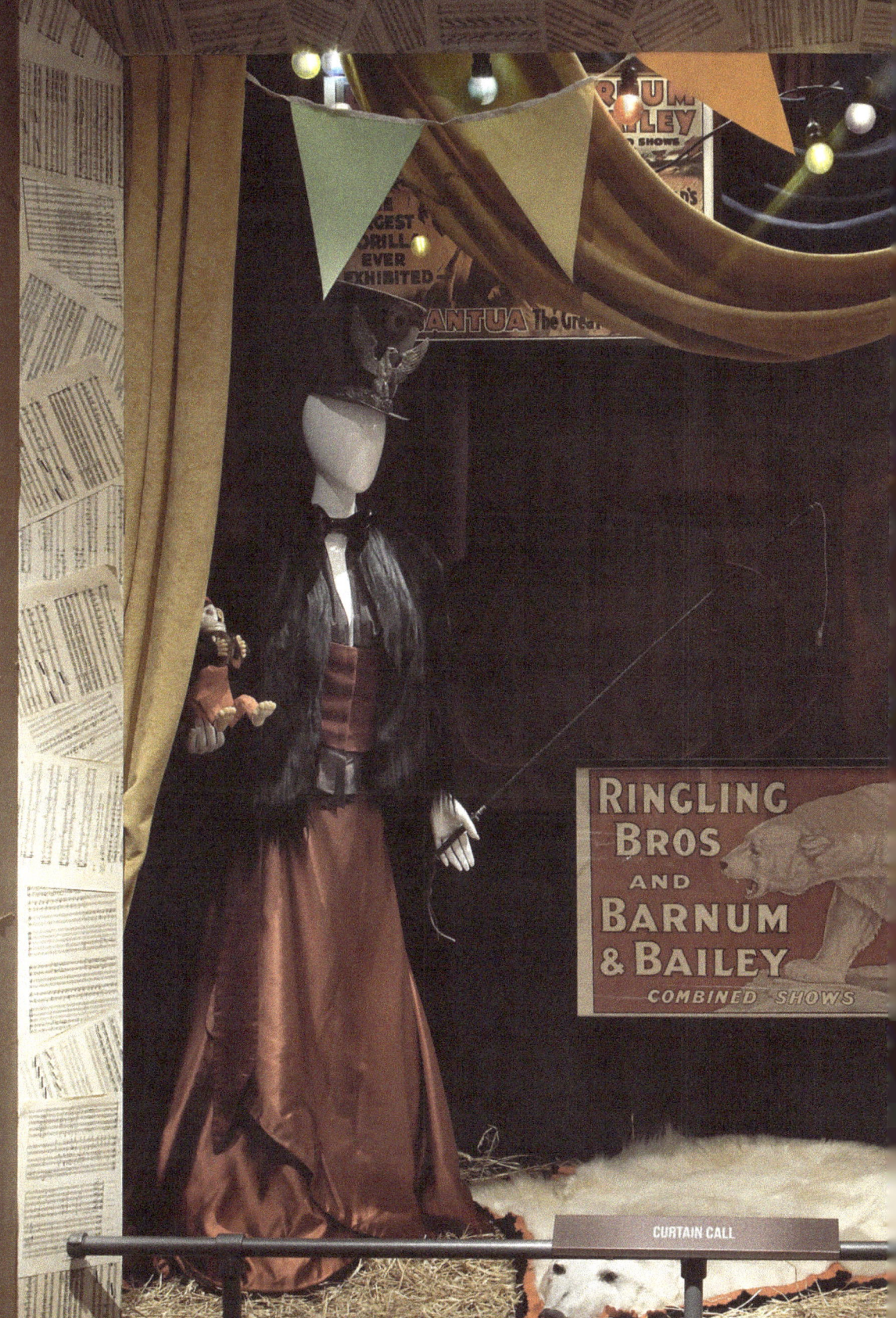

RINGLING BROS AND BARNUM & BAILEY COMBINED SHOWS

CURTAIN CALL

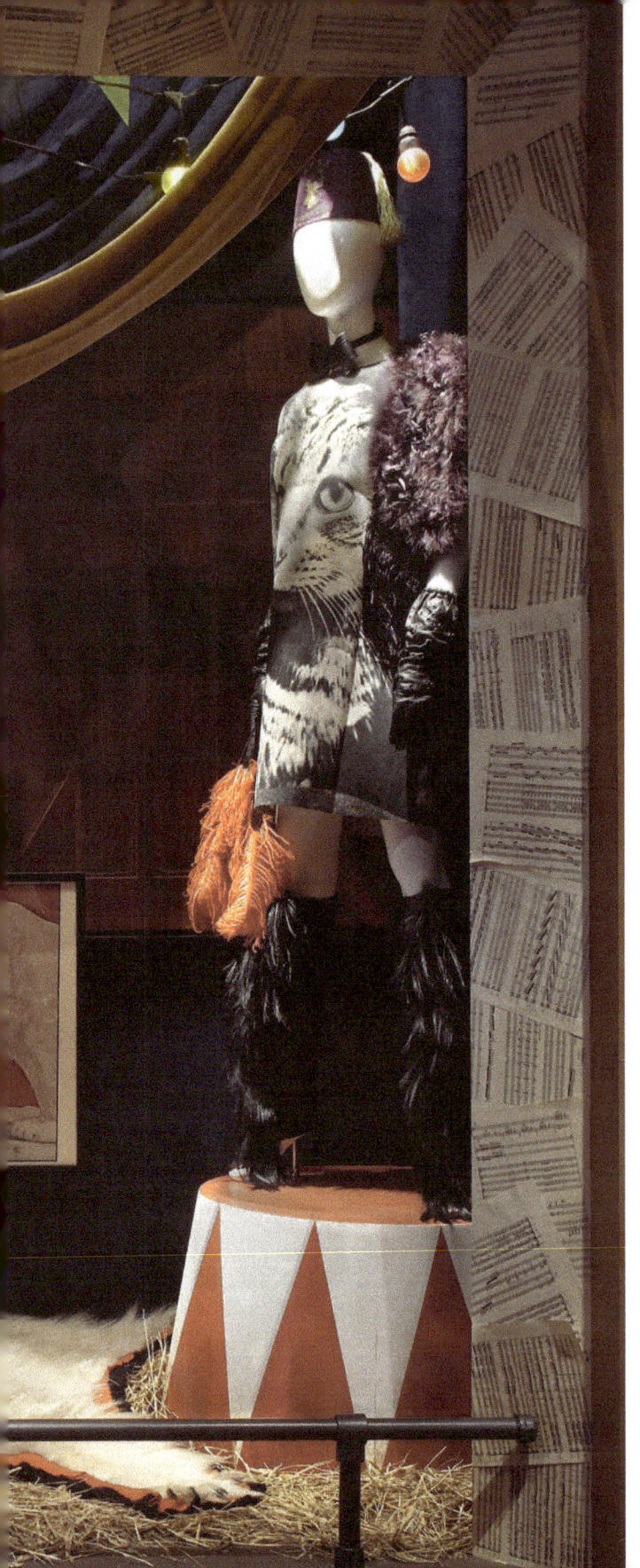

curtain call   The two circus posters from Glenbow's Archives were the first items Paul Hardy chose for this window to represent the popularity of the circus and the excitement surrounding the presentation of exotic animal species. Other items in this window—the coat made of monkey fur, the polar bear rug and the faux cat dress— all represent the eventual demise of the circus as first popularized in the late 1800s.

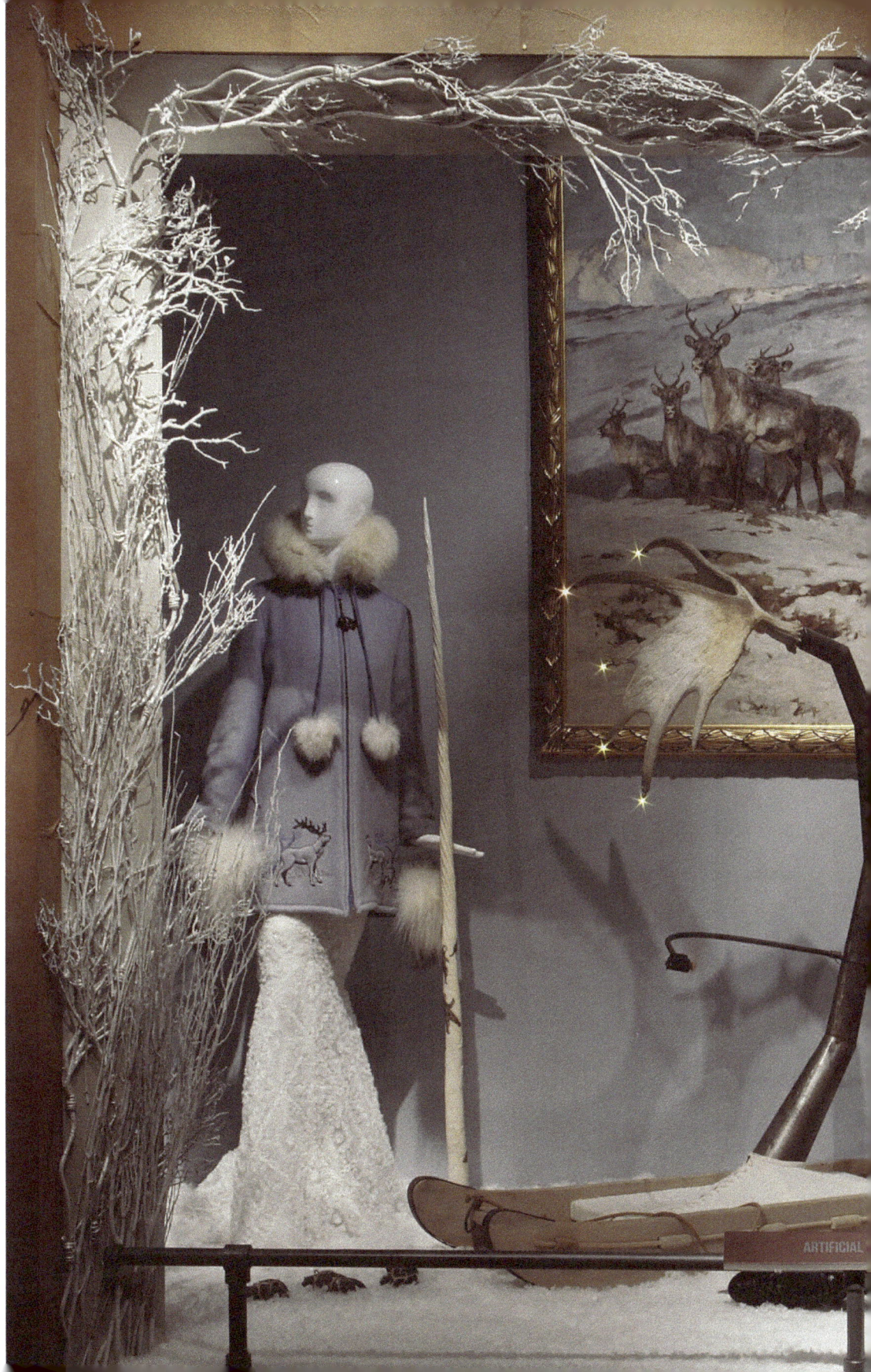

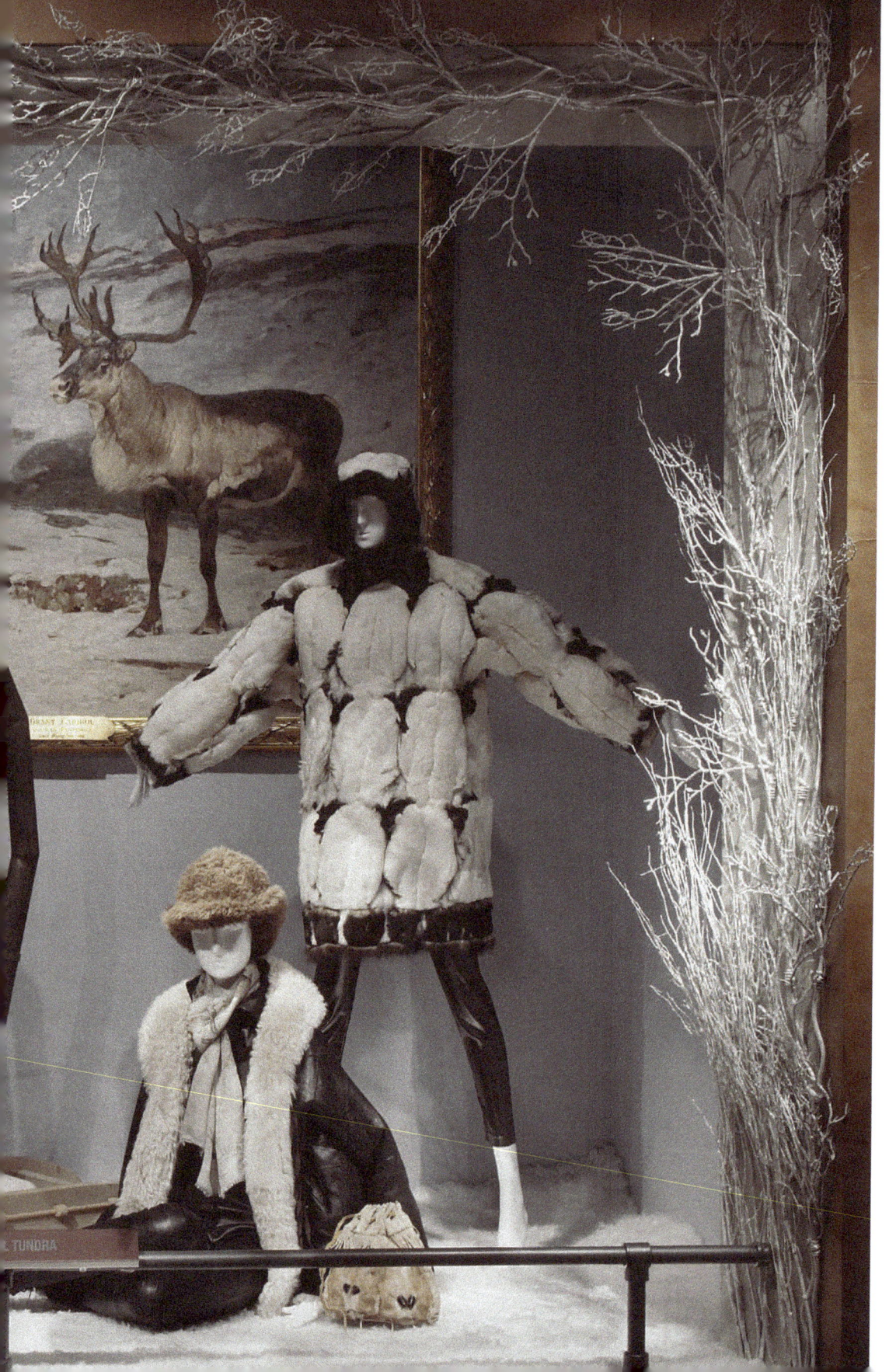

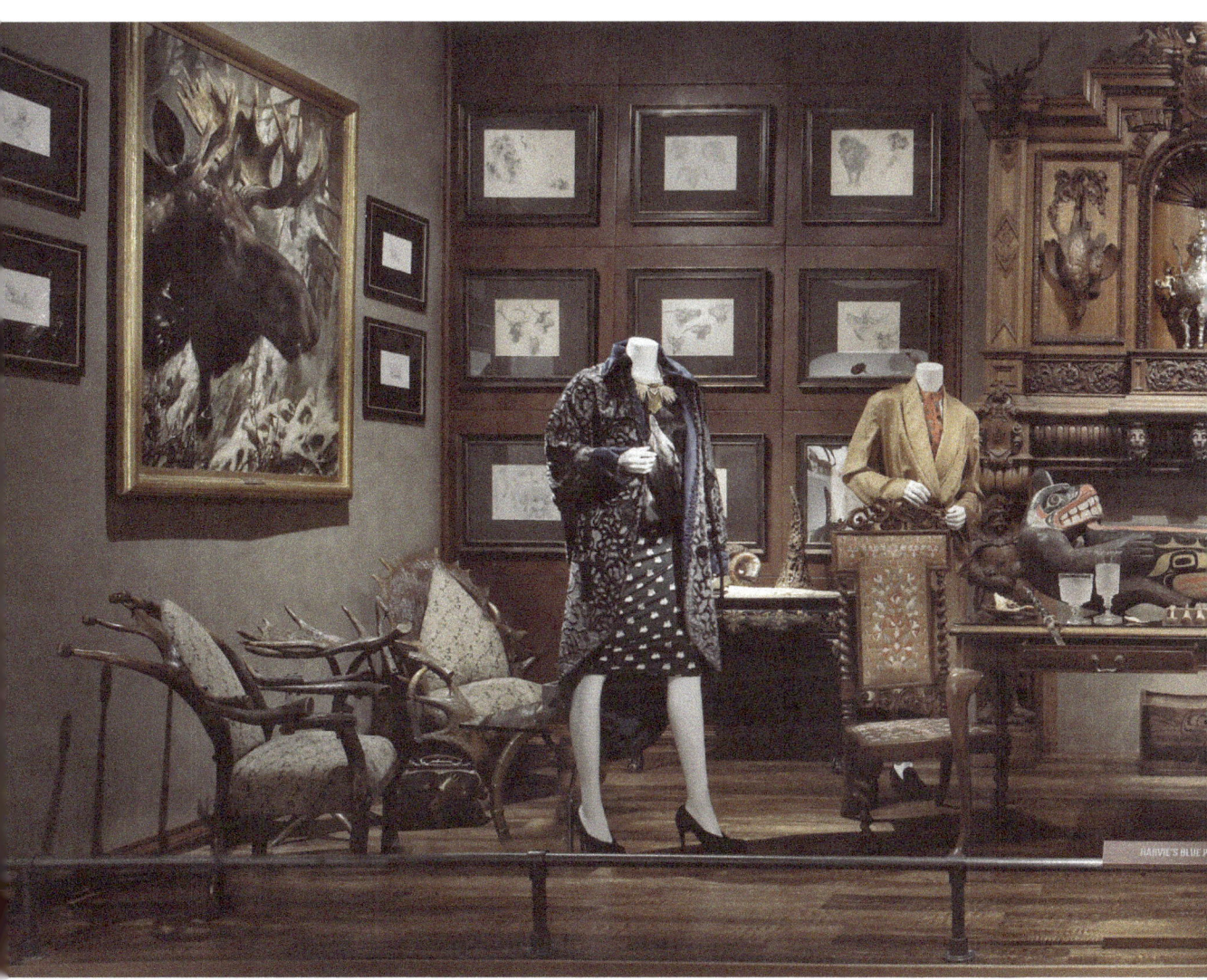

previous
artificial tundra   In this scene on the frozen tundra, a correlation is made between
the functional influences animals have had on fashion design (cold-weather climates
in particular) and demonstrates that this influence transcends cultural lines.

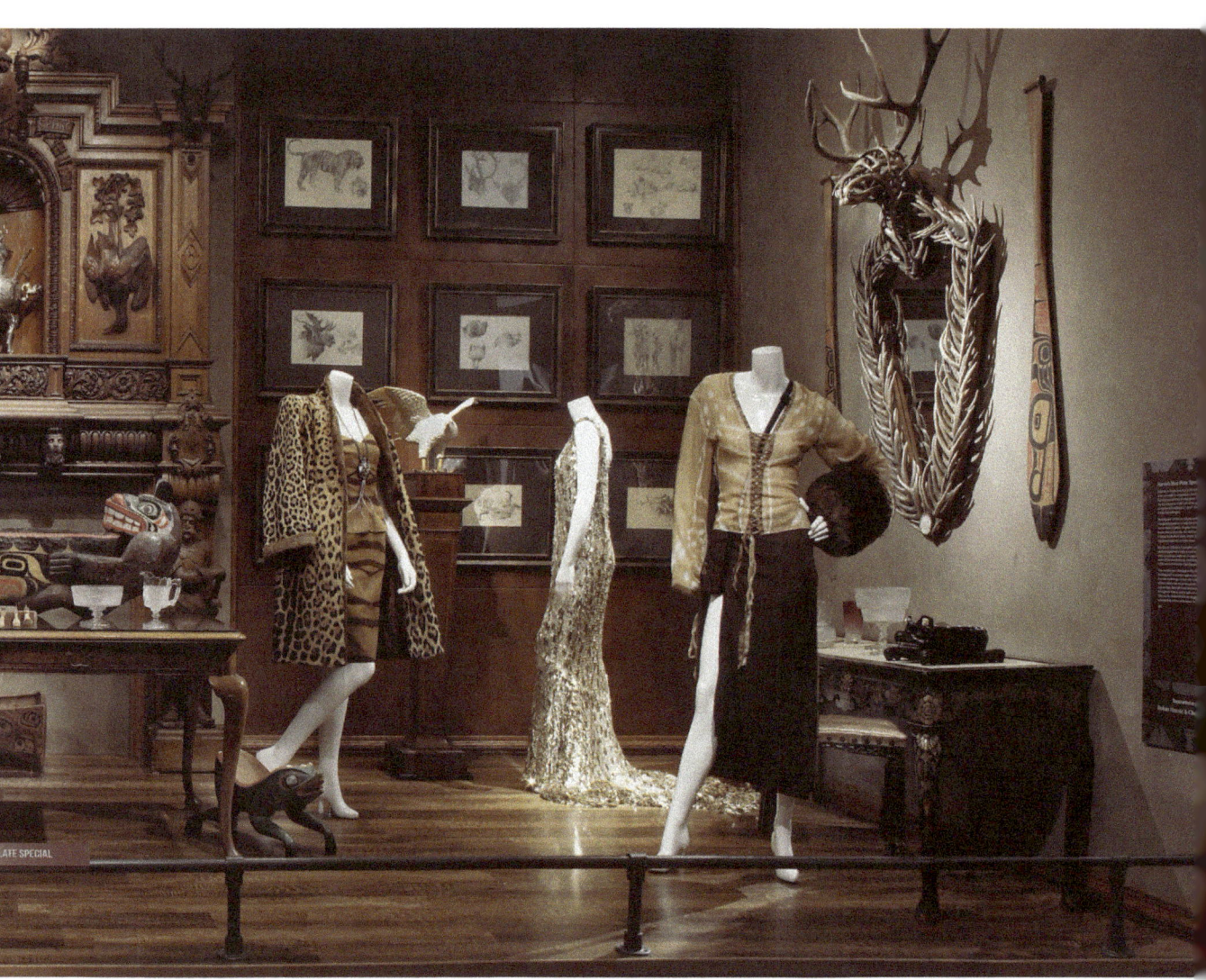

above

harvie's blue plate special   This window pays homage to Eric Harvie—Glenbow's founder —and his interests in wildlife, hunting and his eclectic appreciation for other cultures. It is also an homage to how the common theme of animal subject matter has been integrated into various forms and designs, through both their aesthetics and materials, and throughout history and in cultures around the world. This can be understood in its simplest form, through communing over a carnivorous meal.

lisa brawn interview

Artist Lisa Brawn has been a vital part of the Calgary art scene for over twenty years, as a founding member of collectives such as United Congress and Sugar. Brawn has worked in a variety of media, including installation art, but the largest part of her practice is woodcut portraits, most often on thick blocks of salvaged Douglas fir. Rather than using the woodcuts to make prints, Brawn paints the woodcuts themselves, producing strikingly graphic images. One major group of woodcuts consists of series of portraits of pop culture icons, such as movie monsters, country singers, artists, and musicians.

portfolio
calgary institute for the humanities

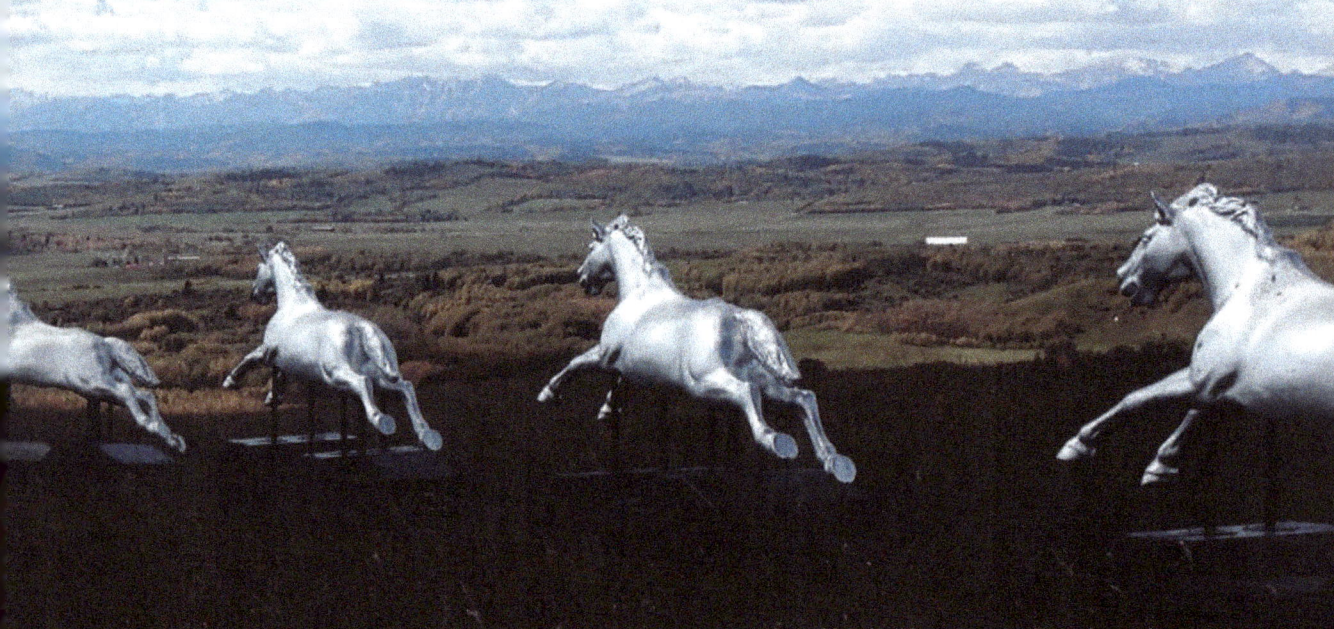

The other major group are portraits of wild birds. These works have been featured on City of Calgary banners, in a bestselling 2015 Andrews McMeel calendar, in Calgary's Festival Hall, and in many other places. Brawn's 2016 show in Austin, Texas, at the Yard Dog Art Gallery, *¿Quién Es Más Macho?*, brought together her two major portrait subjects, pairing exotic characters from the films of Wes Anderson with wild birds of Texas. Most recently she has received acclaim for her 2016 installation *Helios* at the Leighton Art Centre, which involved a "solar-powered, interactive, kinetic sculptural installation consisting of eight large repurposed vintage mechanical horses running wild across the breathtaking prairie landscape."[53] She has described this installation as a "re-wilding" of the ride-on urban horses that used to spend their lives entertaining children outside grocery stores and Woolcos.

CIH: What led you to juxtapose the Wes Anderson characters with the birds of Texas?

Lisa Brawn: I intuited that there was a common thread running through these, and needed to see them side by side to explore that further. First of all, there is an unmistakable fabulousness; any one of them could be a finalist in RuPaul's Drag Race. The Anderson characters have their arsenal of cherry berets, mirrored aviators, striped headbands, and purple pillboxes, while the wild birds of Texas brought their jewel tones represented by green monk parakeets and the blue-green-yellow-red painted buntings. I would also like to submit their names for evidence: Anderson's Oseary Drakoulias and Vladimir Wolodarsky vs. the wild birds *Myiopsitta monachus* and *Passerina ciris* from the family Cardinalidae. *¿Quién es más macho?* is a running theme I have going at Yard Dog gallery in Austin, and these two seemed like worthy adversaries.

CIH: Why are you drawn to wild birds as subject matter?

LB: I have always been preoccupied with birds. I walk a lot and listen for them, and try to find them; for example, if I hear a woodpecker I have to follow the sound until I see him, and then I just stare like a lovesick fool. If a downy is at the suet feeder or a nuthatch is in the maple tree in my yard, the world stops for those ninety seconds or so. They are miniature and mysterious and fantastic, and everywhere to be found. I'm interested in details, so mountains are boring, but I could spend days studying bird nostrils and bristle feathers. It has been a challenge to interpret this information graphically, and the fascination is never-ending.

CIH: Is there any relation of your work to some of the earlier iconic bird illustrators, such as John James Audubon? He was revolutionary in depicting birds in their natural setting; you don't do that, obviously.

LB: No, those are too soft. I have an affinity with delineators such as cloisonnists or ukiyo-e printmakers. My Achilles heel is German Expressionism. It sits in the corner of my mind. One day I will open that Pandora's box but right now I am still doing studies. For the moment it's enough that my birds could kick ass in a bar brawl.

CIH: If you aren't aiming for the same kind of accurate detail that motivated the naturalists, what is important for you to get right? When carving a jay, for example, what are you attempting to convey about the jay?

LB: It is a very unforgiving medium; one wrong cut and it's firewood. It required tremendous stubbornness to master the technique; starting out I had a 98 per cent failure rate. Now, twenty years later, it is rare for a woodcut to go horribly wrong, but still happens 3 per cent of the time. Over the years I have also raised the bar significantly. At the start, it was a miracle to achieve a decent rendering, for example, that is supposed to be a red-winged blackbird, not a baked potato. Now the measure of success is if the woodcut packs a graphic punch, has an interesting composition that traps your eye, if the colours vibrate, and if there is an access point / opportunity to leave your self and inhabit the subject.

CIH: What are the iconic birds of Calgary?

LB: The usual suspects are magpies, chickadees, crows, sparrows, pigeons, swallows, blackbirds, finches, ducks and geese, gulls, hawks, falcons . . . and I would have to add downy woodpeckers, northern flickers, waxwings, and nuthatches.
See, I almost forgot ROBINS.

CIH: Is there a particular bird that for you really sums up Calgary?

LB: For me, it's the black-capped chickadee. They don't seem to care how cold it is. They are handsome, clever, observant, cheerful, and they just go about their business.

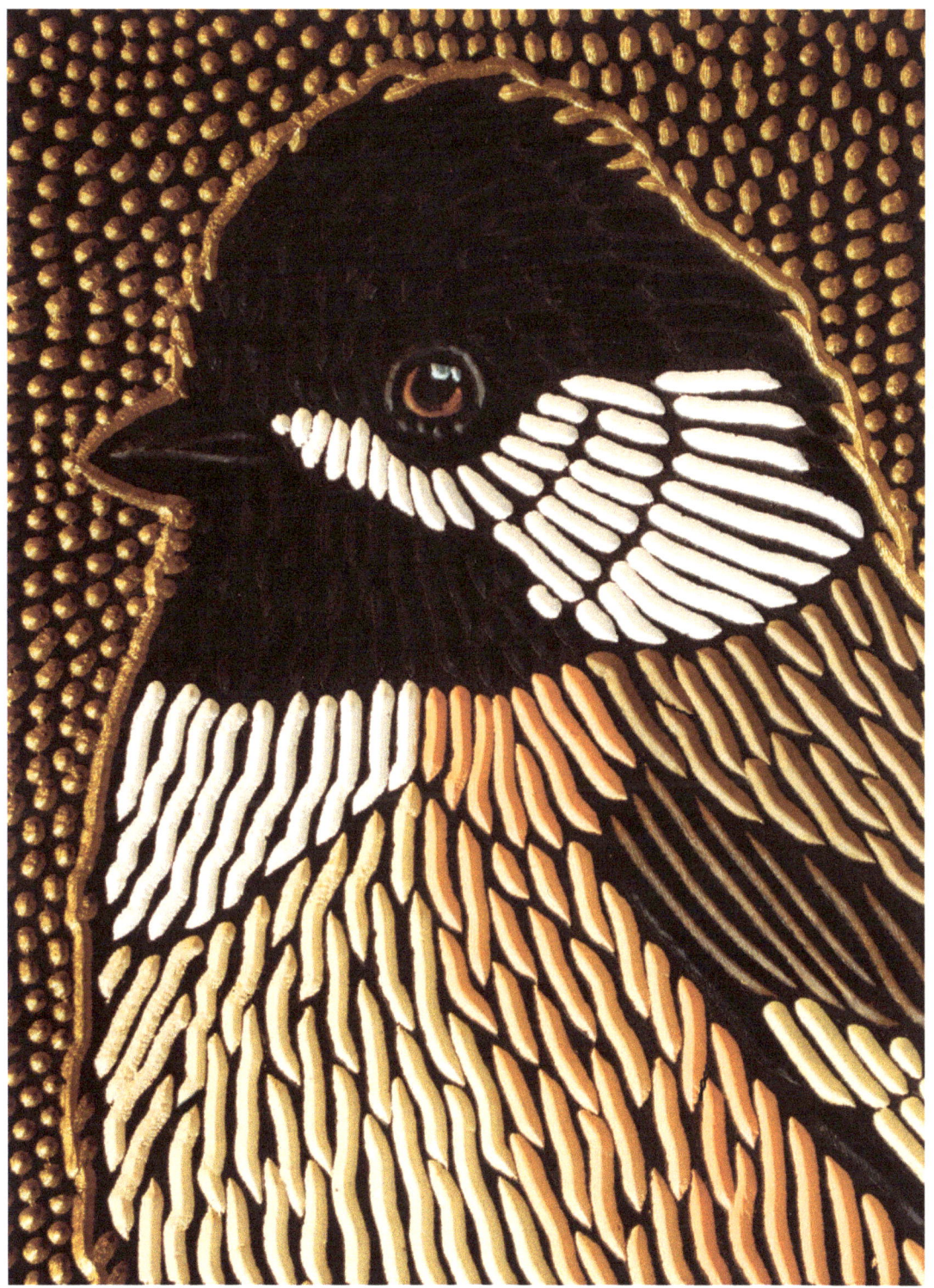

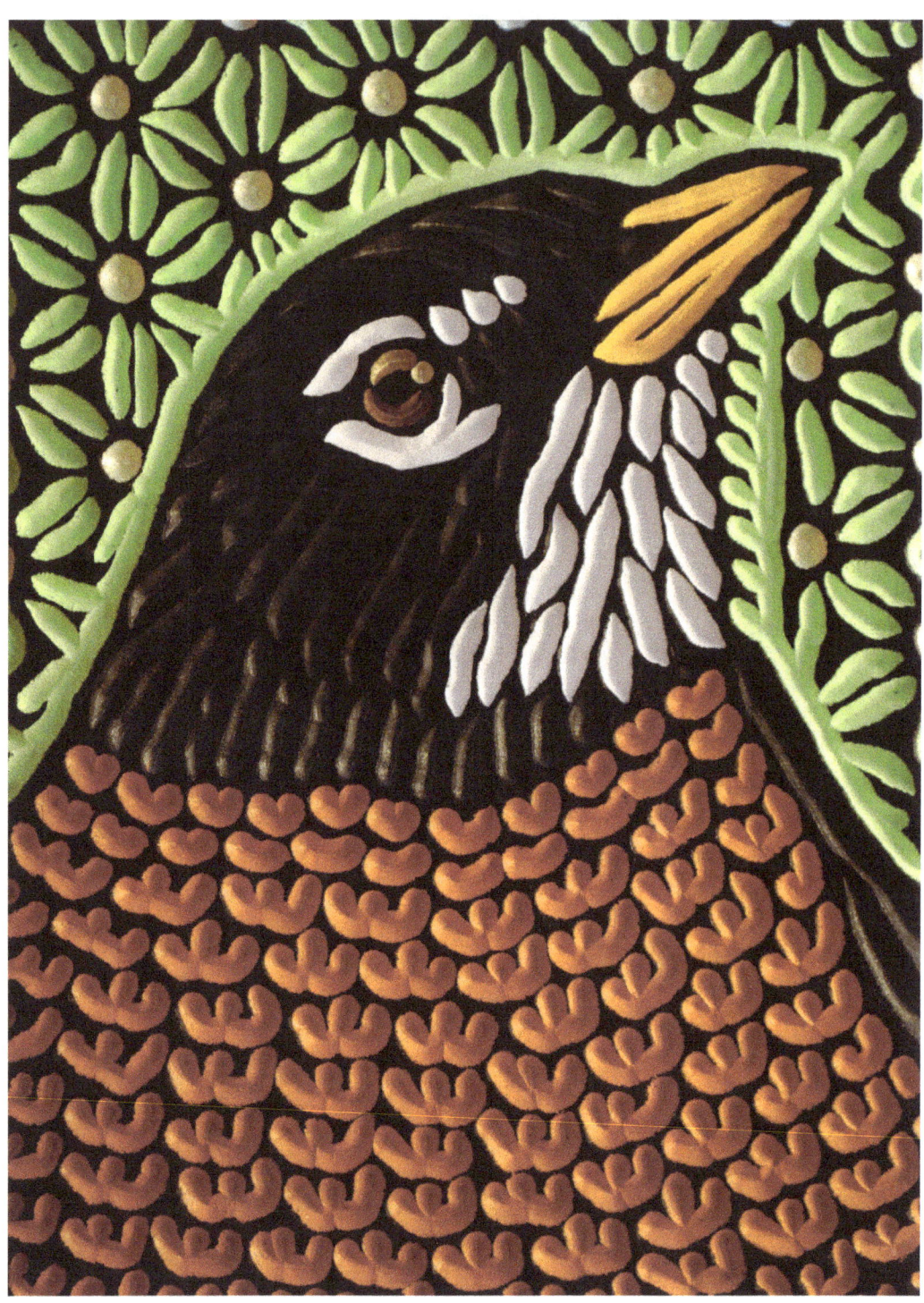

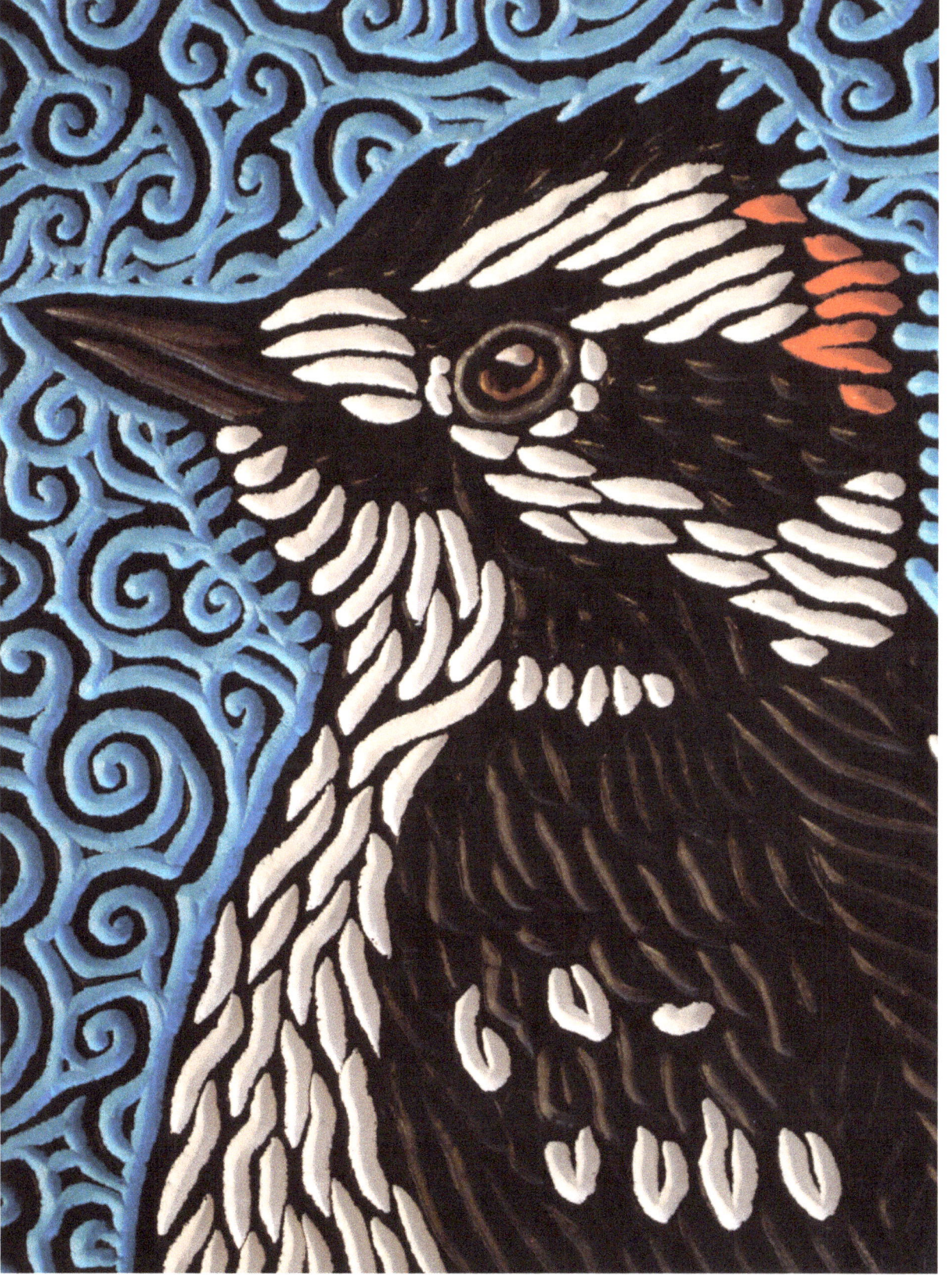

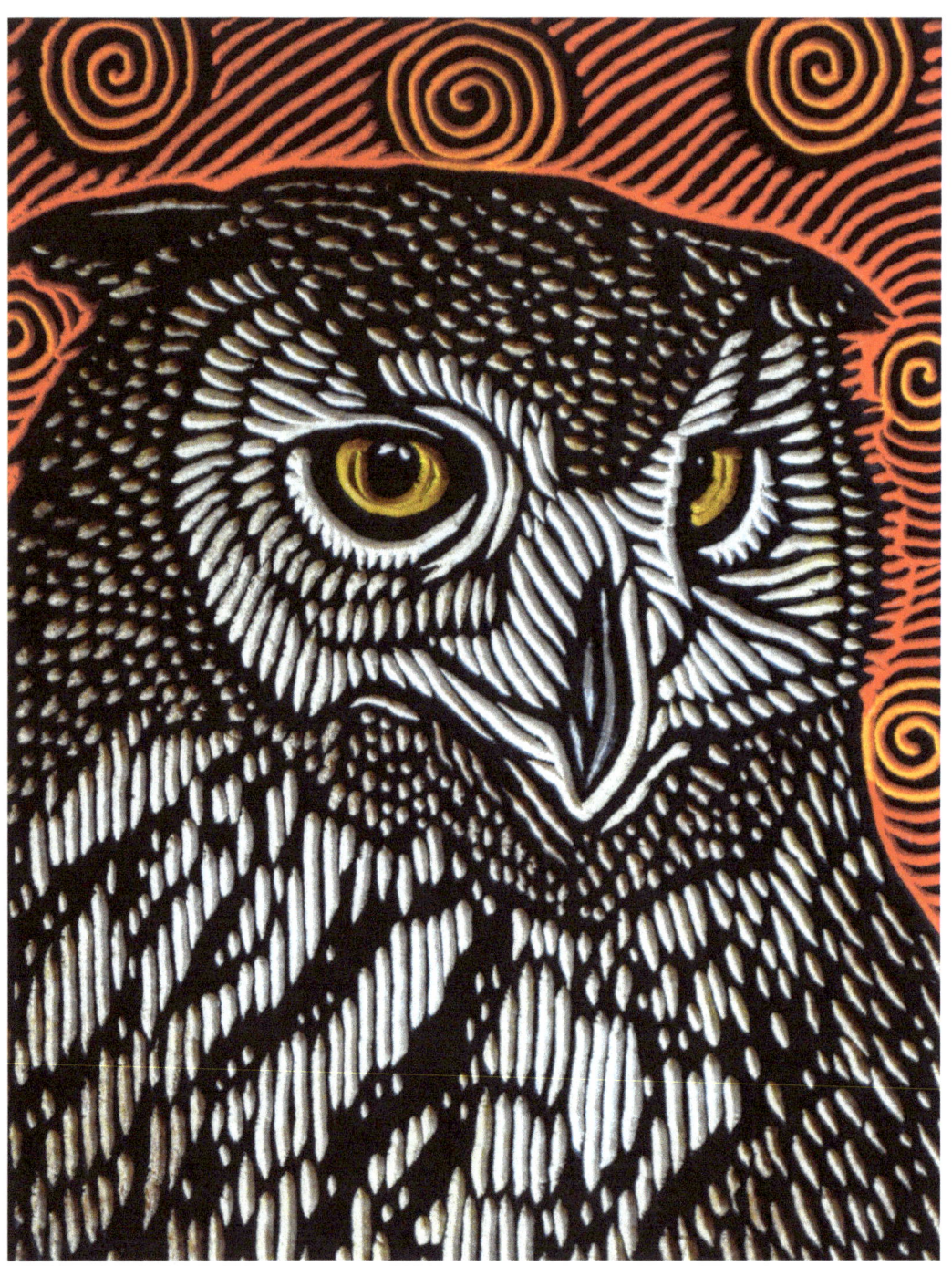

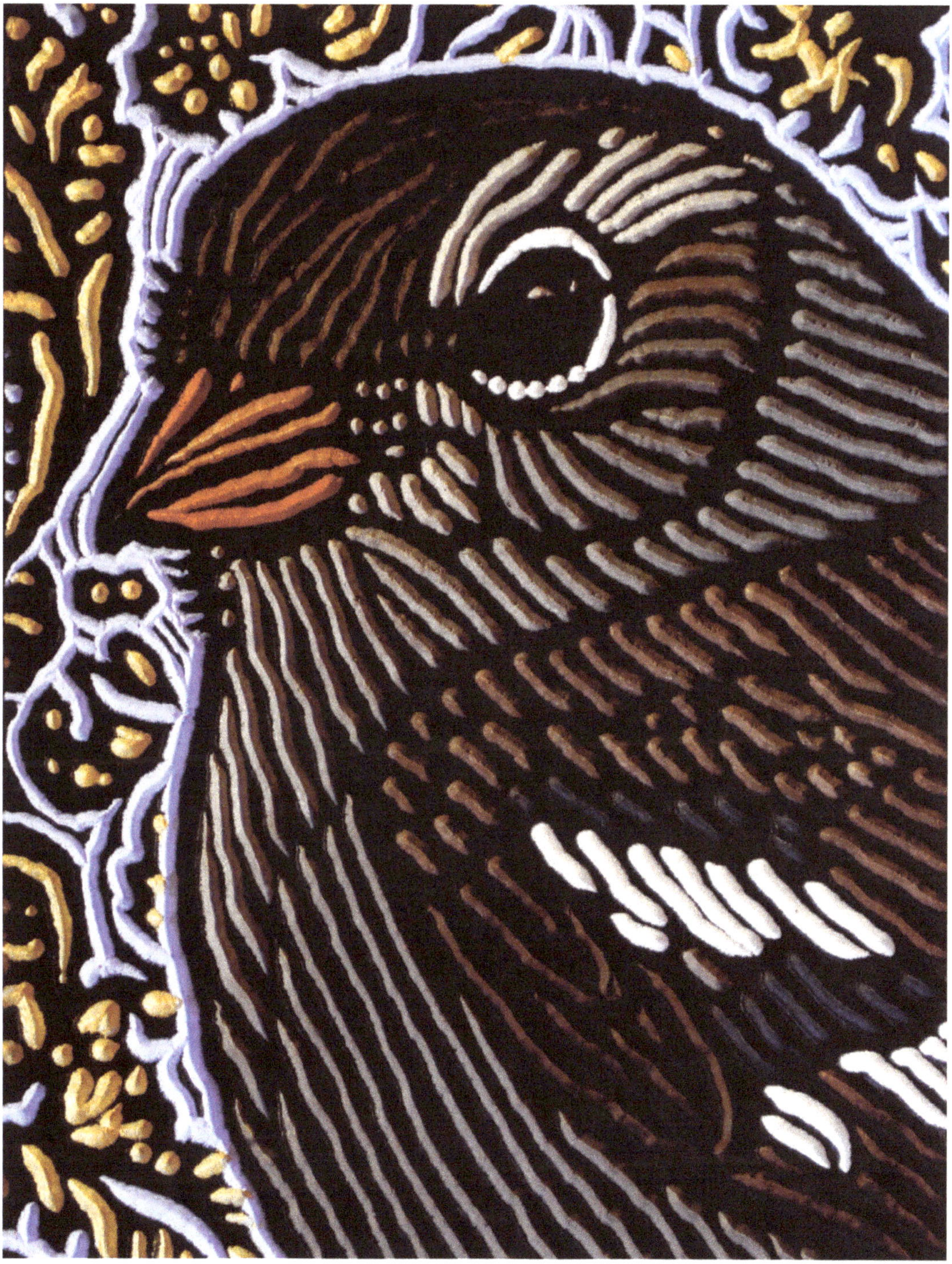

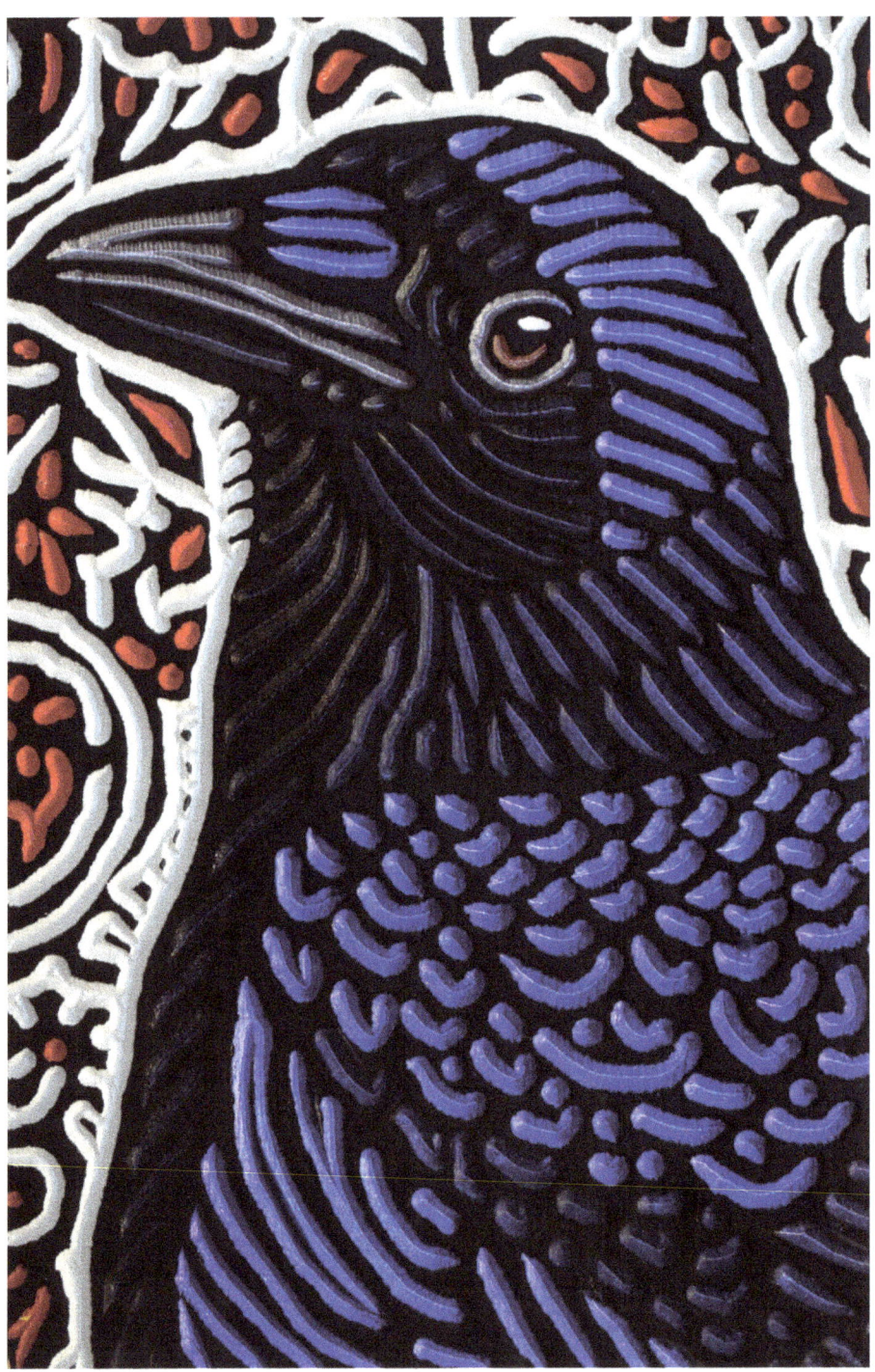

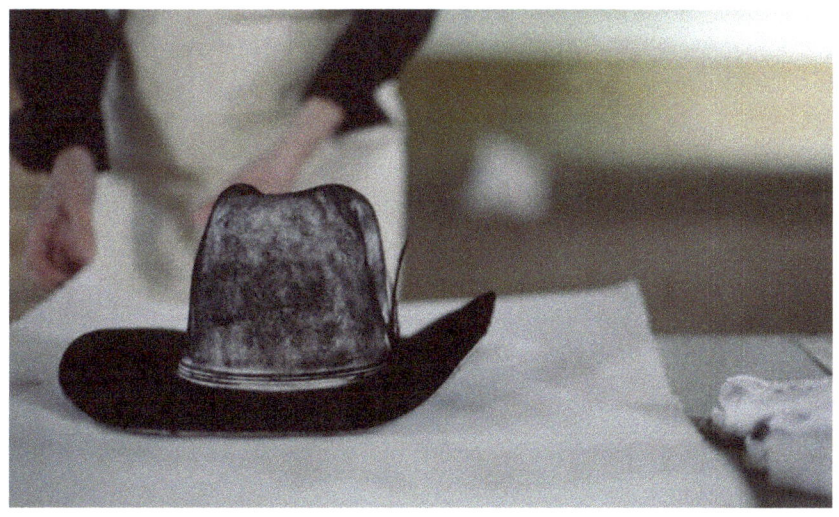

her dark materials

yvonne mullock's
dark horse at stride gallery

jim ellis
university of calgary

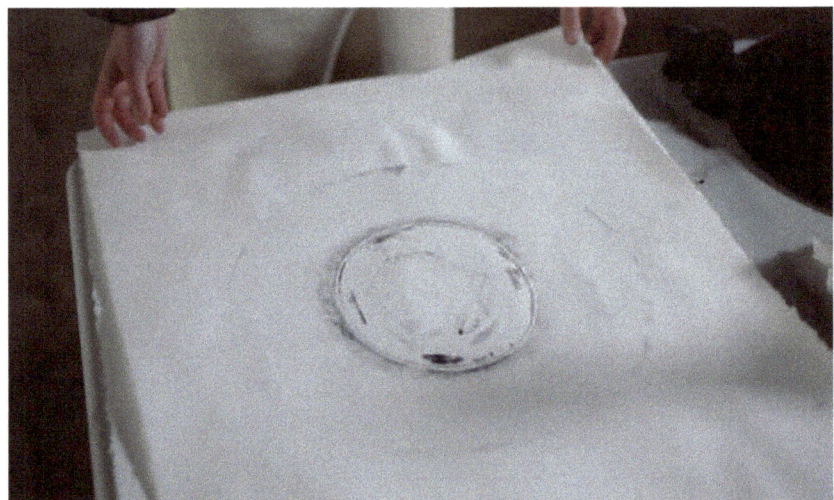
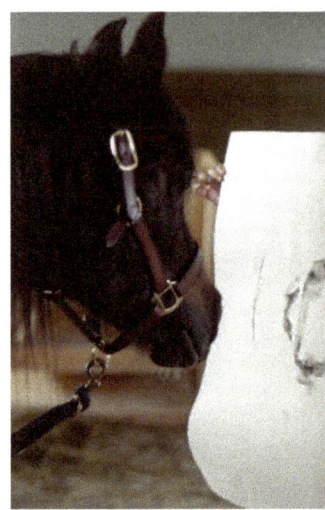

Yvonne Mullock's *Dark Horse* ran from June 3 to July 15 at Calgary's Stride Gallery, overlapping the dates of the 2016 Calgary Stampede. The installation consisted of three principal parts: a set of paired, framed monoprints of the top and bottom of a flattened cowboy hat; the press constructed to make these prints, which uses the weight of a horse to crush the hat; and a video that documents the production of the artworks. The press (fabricated by Ann Thrale) resembles the sort of treadmill formerly used in farms that were powered by horses or large dogs; in its dimensions, it is about the size of the animal chutes used at the Stampede. It has an inclined platform that is attached to pulleys, and gates at both the back and the front. Attached to the front gate is a trough that holds hay. The video (shot by Noel Bégin, and approximately sixteen minutes long) takes us through the production of two sets of prints. Although ostensibly it works to document the process-as-performance, it is itself shot and edited in a highly artful way that directs the viewer's attention to all of the various animate and inanimate elements of the art-making assemblage.

In the video, the action takes place in a riding stable. In the middle of the corral are a couple of tables with hats, ink, and paper, while nearby sits the printing press, with ropes extending from it to weights. A figure in a white apron (Mullock) enters, walks to the table, opens a can of ink and spreads it on some paper with a palette knife. She then rollers and sponges the ink onto a hat, and puts the hat between two sheets of paper that have been sprayed with water. The paper and hat are carefully placed in the press.

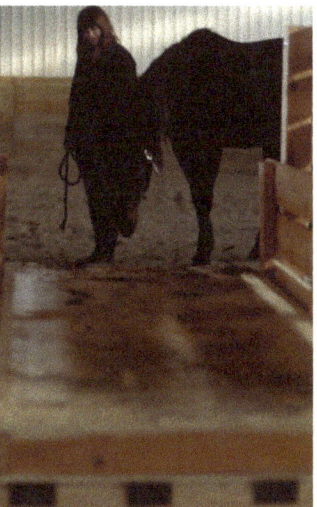
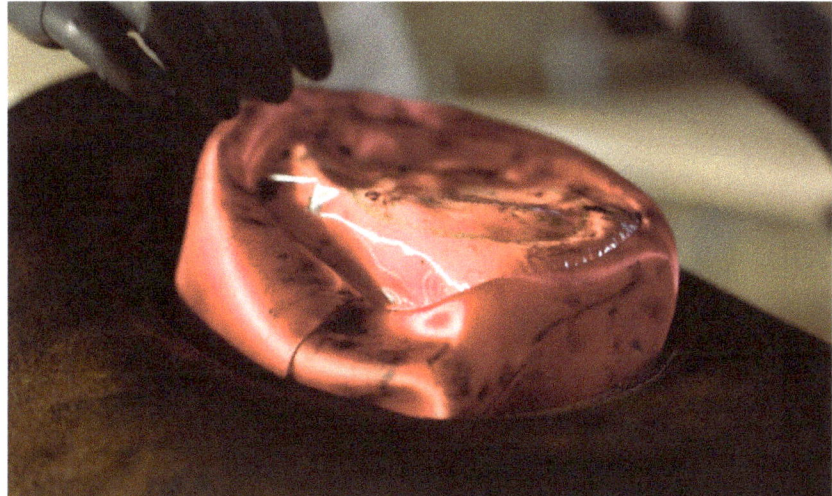

A horse (Shere Kaan) is led by a handler (Karly Mortimer) up to the press; it steps onto the platform and begins to eat the hay. The platform lowers, and the hat is flattened. When the hay has been eaten, the front gate is opened and the horse steps gingerly out. The print is removed and displayed to the horse, who in the first iteration has no reaction. The process is repeated. On a second viewing, the horse appears to nuzzle the print, and the printmaker looks delighted. Otherwise, there is little emotion to be seen in the video.

There is an obvious comedy to this process and to this machine, which is not unlike the elaborate contraptions made by Wile E. Coyote to capture (or obliterate) the ever-elusive roadrunner. In those cartoons, the coyote was, like the stetson hats here, frequently flattened into an imprint. He became a representation of the violence that he tried to visit on the roadrunner but which is instead returned to his own body: the flattened coyote as the sign of an ironic poetic justice. Here, we might be tempted to see the press as the horse's symbolic revenge on the cowboy, on behalf of all the horses who were pressed into the service of the Stampede, and in compensation for whatever suffering they endured. As Susan Nance shows in her essay in this collection, Stampede horses were made to serve as signs of something other than themselves. In Mullock's work the crushed stetson, a key symbol of the cowboy and the west, could be read as the sign of the horse's revenge.

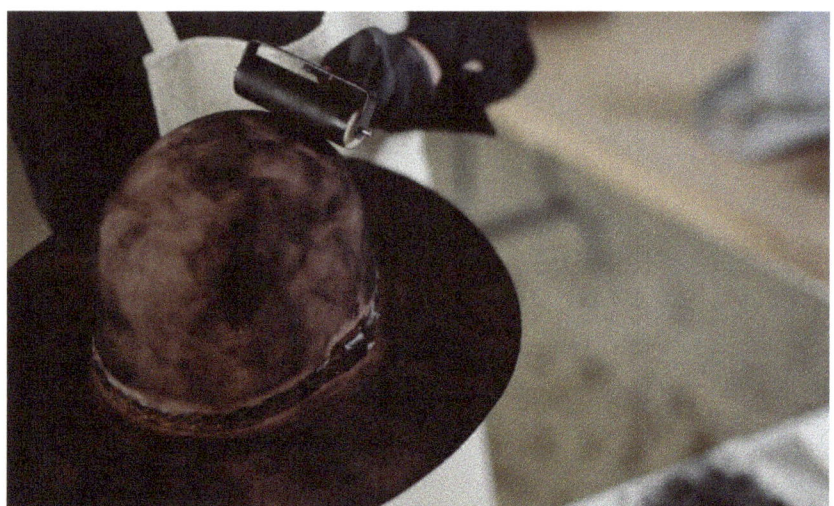
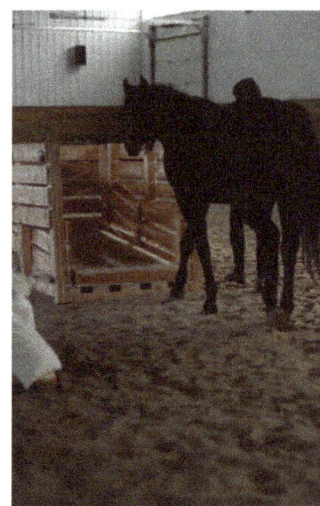

When we watch the video, however, it is difficult to see any spirit of revenge at work, because the horse appears neither to understand nor to care about the art being produced. This is reminiscent of one of the crucial elements of the Wile E. Coyote dramas: their asymmetry. The coyote was recognizably human, with a human name and human emotions. He was obsessed with the roadrunner, with a desire that went far beyond the need for nourishment. The roadrunner, on the other hand, was largely without emotion. He occasionally displayed what could be labelled an animal curiosity, and at times, he showed what seemed like a fleeting amusement at the futility of the coyote's obsessions and the inevitability of his failure. But his joy largely stemmed from his own animal motion, and he never entered into the human realm the way the coyote did, with Wile E.'s elaborately drawn plans and his frequent orders to the Acme Corporation. Crucially, the roadrunner did not have a name, which placed him beyond the borders of the human. He was unlike almost every other animal in the cartoon universe in retaining his alterity. This made him a frustrating presence, putting us to some degree in the same camp as the anthropomorphized coyote: we could only ever guess what might be going on in his head.

In writing about art that addresses animal rights and animal welfare, or what is often called the "question of the animal," the theorist of post-humanism Cary Wolfe (2010) urges us to think about the formal strategies of the art, rather than just the content. He looks at Sue Coe's drawings of the faces of animals in slaughterhouses, and how these

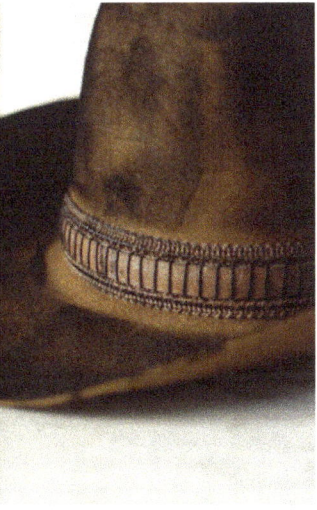 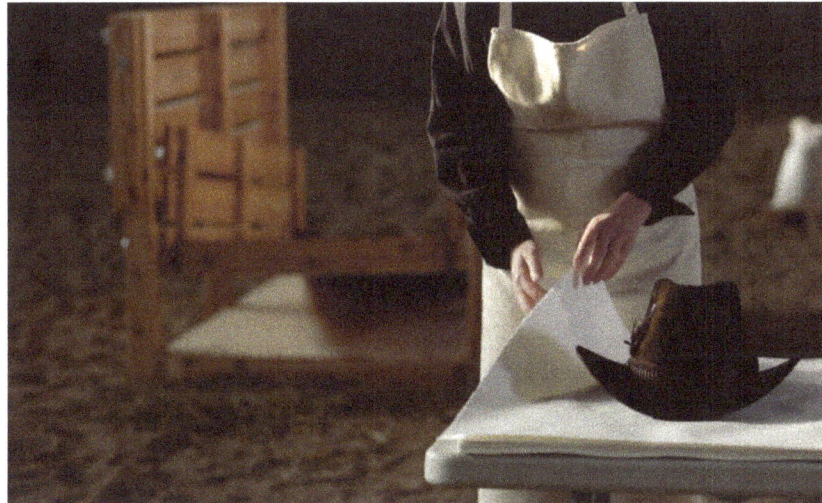

representations work to generate empathy. But he argues that their effectivity to some degree hinges on the way the animal faces in her art evoke a human face, with a human-like consciousness and human-like suffering implied. This is similar to certain arguments for animal rights or the ethical standing of animals: that animals are like us, and therefore our concept of rights should be expanded to include them in our circle. The limitation of this way of thinking is precisely the problem of limits: How far can we or do we extend our compassion or our fellow-feeling? Does it go further than those beings we can readily anthropomorphize? More fundamentally, it leaves the human in the centre, as the measure of everything. It does not challenge us to rethink what it means to be human, and in particular, how the human has been defined in relation to the animal, but rather extends to non-human animals key aspects of humanity. In the process, it could be argued, it fails to recognize or respect the animalness or the alterity of the animal. Put another way: the effectivity of this kind of art is the extent to which it can remake the animal in human terms.

Rather than generating sympathy through the representation of rodeo horses or other animals, Mullock's work pushes us to attend to the processes that make art. Rather than picturing animals, she has in a series of works involved animals in the production of images or objects or performances. In *Dog Pick-Up Sticks*, for example, a performance made with Ann Thrale, dogs play a game with huge pick-up sticks made from poles. There is an aleatory element of this work that is different from the print-making process:

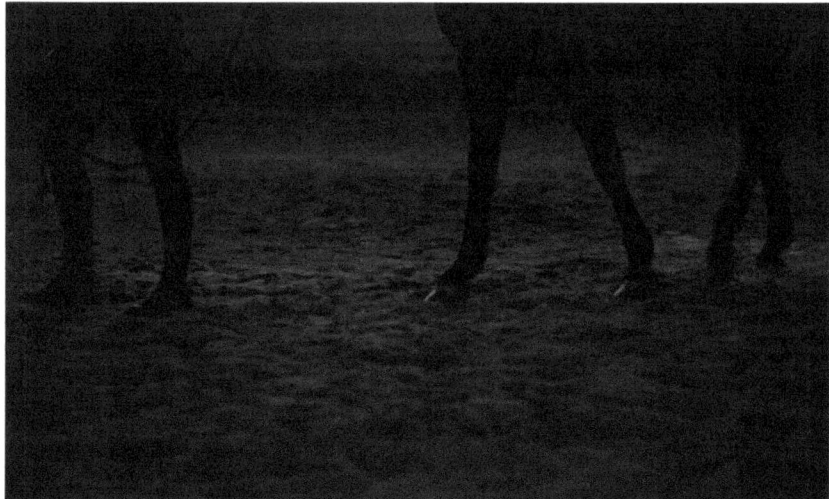

pp 104-109 photos by Noel Bégin

the final work is unpredictable, as it is produced by chance. This work prompts us to question in what sense or to what extent the animals are participating in the act of creation, as animals. What does it mean to think of an animal as an artist, or a co-creator of art? The most naïve formulation of this would be to claim that the paint marks made by animals on canvas or paper are art, and that the animal is an artist, which remakes the animal in human terms. By contrast, this video suggests that art is fairly meaningless to a horse. But is it possible to see the horse in *Dark Matter* as a co-creator, without overwriting its animal nature?

The video offers us few different approaches to this question. Two immediate things to note are that there are no credits, and there is no language anywhere in the video. Language has long been used as one of the key dividing lines between the human and the non-human, and so the lack of language arguably enacts a kind of levelling between the various beings in the video. The lack of credits takes this further, and highlights one of the central issues explored in the work: Who and what should be credited with the creation of this work of art? Who or what makes any work of art possible? In expanding our sense of co-creators, we might think beyond the inclusion of the trio of animate beings at the centre of the work—the artist, the horse, and its handler—and also consider the inanimate objects that together make the assemblage that produces the print: surely the hay that lures the horse to the press is a crucial part of the process, as are the prominently displayed weights that allow the press's motion, as is of course the press itself.

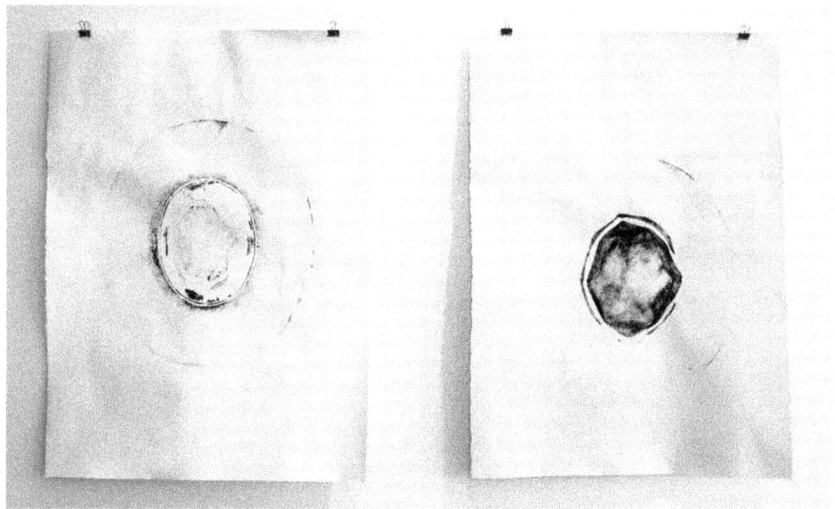

Attention to the conjunction of beings and objects that produces the work takes us past the human/animal divide, to consider the more fundamental division between animate and inanimate. Here we enter the realm of what Jane Bennett calls the universe of "vibrant matter." In her materialist view of the universe, Bennett goes back to the classical philosopher Lucretius, who argued that everything in existence is made of the same atoms, and the most fundamental creative power in the universe is the ability of these atoms to swerve and collide, creating new forms. Matter, in this view, is not inert. While not ascribing intention or volition to matter and material things, Bennett urges us to think of objects as "actants," as agents that help to make things happen. We need to be attentive, she argues, to "the agentic contributions of nonhuman forces" (Bennett 2010, xvi) that form part of the assemblages of beings and objects that come together to cause events or produce effects. As with Animal Studies, this attention to the web of connections between human, animal, and material actants has an ethical dimension: it insists that we are all part of the same material web, created out of the same atoms, and thus we have an ethical duty to consider the non-human and even the inanimate when thinking about the implications of our actions in the world.

This might seem like a large weight to put on a video of a horse crushing a hat, a video whose overall affect is best characterized as droll. This droll affect is in fact crucial in orienting us toward the performance: it encourages a distanced, bemused perspective on all of the actors and actants. Part of the drollness is created by the sound, which is

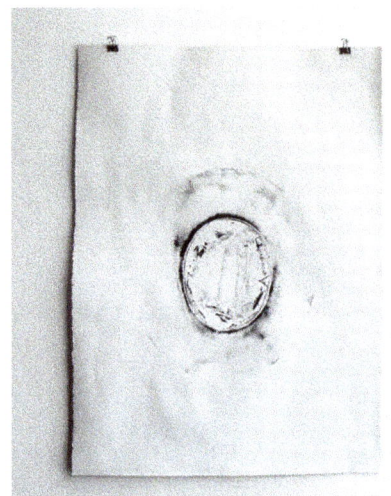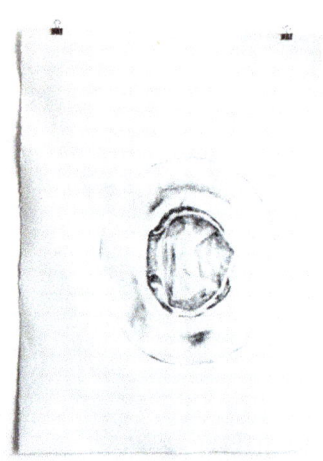

pp 110-111 photos by Nicole Kelly Westman

a crucial element in the video's attention to the work of representation and, in particular, the representation of matter and material relations. The video has something of the mood of a Buster Keaton silent comedy, with a musicality to the sound track created by rhythmic motion that underscores the video's essentially comic nature. We hear the quick back-and-forth rhythm of the roller on the sticky inked paper; the repeated daubing of a sponge on the hat; the quick sharp sprays of water on the paper. In the absence of any spoken language in the film, these sounds take on a greater prominence than they normally would. With the exception of the horse snorting at the end of the film, virtually all of the sounds are produced by one object coming into contact with another.

One object encountering the border of another creates a sound. Sound presses on our eardrums. We receive an impression. This process is analogous to the mechanical process of creating the print. In the video, we hear the sounds of paper moving on paper, of hoof on wood, of paper pulled across a gritty surface, of hay being stuffed into a wooden trough. We hear the banging when the platform is lowered, and the squeak when it lifts. The dominance of non-linguistic sounds draws attention to the objectness of the entire assemblage; each actant plays its role, with the sound making us aware of how and when each actant encounters another. No one actant makes a sound that is qualitatively different from any other: there is no hierarchy of linguistic and non-linguistic sounds. Rather, these are the sounds the assemblage of actants makes when it produces art.

The horse is an important part of the assemblage that creates the work, but crucially, the horse does not leave its mark on the resulting prints. The print does not record the intention or the emotion of the horse; it is the product of the complex functioning of a series of objects coming into contact with each other: horse on platform; platform on paper; paper on hat; hat on paper. While it provides the force that crushes the hat, the horse's relation to the print is highly mediated. Its trajectory is different from that of the artist: it is led to the platform, and it is rewarded with hay. It knows nothing of the of the hat beneath the platform. The horse retains its horseness; while it might be a co-creator, it is in the more limited (but important) sense of being an actant in an assemblage.

But if the horse's status as co-creator is thus limited, so is that of the human artist. (In an interview with *Canadian Art*, Mullock says that she is simply acting as a printmaker's assistant in the video, with the horse as the printmaker [Sandals 2016].) As with the horse, her relation to the artwork is mediated. Although she determines the conditions of production, and sets the process in motion, she does not completely determine the outcome. Nor does the resulting print bear any discernible trace of her involvement: the print records the coming together of an inked hat and paper placed under considerable force. The distanced, droll tone of the video is again important here: the largely affect-less artist appears more as a technician than a creative, directing force; she appears to be simply performing her preordained functions, like every other part of the assemblage. This is similar to the role played by the artist in those performance pieces like *Dog Pick-Up Sticks*, or the *Beaver Ready Mades*, where Mullock cast in bronze sticks chewed by beavers. The work thus draws attention to the human exceptionalism at work in our notion of art, without making the specious claim that animals can be artists.

To claim that an animal can be an artist can be seen as a form of symbolic violence, making the horse into something that it is not, and thus failing to acknowledge and respect its alterity. In *Dark Matter*, the horse is left to be an animal, while nonetheless participating in the production of meaning. While the entire work makes a comment on the spectacle of violent force that is a crucial element of the entertainment of Stampede, the work itself is paradoxically very gentle. The horse's movements are calm and slow, the handler is bemused, and the artist is mostly clinical in her movements. Although the print is the result of the destruction of the hat through the application of a powerful force, the resulting image is not one that suggests violence; as the essay that accompanied the exhibition noted, the imprints of the pressed hats have a feminine form. The crushing of the hat is an act of symbolic violence that offers a comment on the way that horses have been used for entertainment and work. But crucially, it does this without once again overwriting the horse's horseness by placing it into a different yet equally alienating symbolic position, either positive (artist) or negative (suffering, human-like victim). The video's attention to the various actants that make up the art-making assemblage relieves the horse of the burden of intentionality. The crushing of the hat is not the horse's victory over the cowboy, a symbolic gesture that would be hollow compensation for the way horses have suffered for human entertainment (while providing yet more entertainment). But the horse doesn't care about the hat, or the symbolism it provides. It is not interested in revenge. The horse is a part of the assemblage which makes visible a critique, but this is not the horse's critique. The horse remains a horse, and the absence of any payback does not relieve the human observer of any complicity in our culture's treatment of animals.

works cited

Bennett, Jane. 2010. *Vibrant Matter: A Political Ecology of Things*. Durham, NC: Duke University Press.

Sandals, Leah. 2016. "Yvonne Mullock and the New Stampede Aesthetics," *Canadian Art*. Summer. http://canadianart.ca/features/yvonne-mullock-new-stampede-aesthetics/.

Wolfe, Cary. 2010. *What is Posthumanism?* Minneapolis: Minnesota University Press.

conclusion
jim ellis

The humanities as a discipline (or disciplines) have been defined in various ways, but central to most formulations is the idea that the humanities foster a conversation about what it means to be human. Animal Studies, as these essays have shown, have the potential to shift the terms of that conversation in significant ways. The designation "non-human animals," which several contributors use, shows one such fundamental change. If philosophers since Plato have used animals to help define what it means to be human, they have generally done this with the assumption that animals are fundamentally different from us: that there is a firm border between the animal world and the human world. This division is clearly reflected in the surprise that many people felt on first encountering the phrase "city of animals." Animals (except for pets, of course) are supposed to live in nature. Cities are for people. Animals found in cities are interlopers or pests.

Increasingly, Animal Studies (among other disciplines) have been pushing us to consider how we humans are a part of the animal world and the natural world; this is an increasingly important question in the face of our changing climate. Other philosophers, responding to humanity's domination of the globe, insist that there is no such thing as nature anymore: that everything, animals included, is a part of human culture. We live in the Anthropocene, a geological era of man-made climate change. Either way, we need to consider the ways in which we are a part of the animal world, and they are a part of ours, since we share the same fate.

This is one reason why the humanities are so important in our current moment. The conversation that took place at our Annual Community Seminar, and which is the origin of this volume, brought together a diverse group of citizens to discuss together how we might better understand our relation to the non-human animals with whom we share our city. This book continues that conversation and broadens it, by including new directions and new perspectives, which mutually inform each other. The essays by the seminar participants provide some scholarly directions for discussion; the statements by those who work for animal well-being help us to better understand the facts on the ground (and in the water, and in the air). The various contributions by artists are research in a different form: artists use different channels of exploration and communication to allow us to understand these issues in more visceral ways. Artists show us that animals don't just inhabit our city: they inhabit our imaginations, our bodies, our movements, and our souls. To be attentive to the welfare of animals is to be attentive to the welfare of our selves.

If you'd like to explore any of these ideas further, we have assembled some resources on the website of the Calgary Institute for the Humanities (http://arts.ucalgary.ca/cih/), at the University of Calgary. There you will find a critical vocabulary, detailed suggestions for reading, and links to community organizations. You can also find videos of the talks from the Community Seminar, as well as video of some of the conversations that took place. We hope you will be inspired to carry on the conversation: let us know where it takes you.

notes

[1] *Our BiodiverCity: Calgary's 10-year Biodiversity Strategic Plan*, http://www.calgary.ca/CSPS/Parks/Documents/Planning-and-Operations/Biodi-verCity-strategic-plan.pdf.

[2] *Totemism*, trans. Rodney Needham (Boston: Beacon Press, 1963), 89.

[3] "Backyard Chicken Pilot Project Scratched by Calgary Council," *CBC News*, last modified April 27, 2015, http://www.cbc.ca/news/canada/calgary/backyard-chicken-pilot-project-scratched-by-calgary-council-1.3050684.

[4] Jason Markusoff, "No to Hen-Raisers: Council Votes Against a Backyard Chicken Coop Pilot Program" *Calgary Herald*, last modified April 27, 2015, http://calgaryher-ald.com/news/local-news/no-to-hen-raisers-council-votes-against-a-backyard-coop-pilot-program.

[5] "Livestock in the city and the Responsible Pet Ownership Bylaw," City of Calgary, http://www.calgary.ca/CSPS/ABS/Pages/Animal-Services/Responsible-pet-owner-ship-bylaw-livestock.aspx.

[6] David Rider, "Toronto Committee Votes to Uphold Backyard Chicken Ban," *Toronto*

Star, last modified January 25, 2012, https://www.thestar.com/news/city_hall/2012/01/25/toronto_committee_votes_to_uphold_backyard_chicken_ban.html.

[7] "Edmonton hatches expanded plans for backyard chickens" *CBC News*, last modified March 7, 2016, http://www.cbc.ca/news/canada/edmonton/edmonton-hatches-expanded-plans-for-backyard-chickens-1.3479115.

[8] "Urban Hens Pilot Evaluation," Report CR_1621 to Community Services Committee, City of Edmonton, March 7, 2016, http://sirepub.edmonton.ca/sirepub/cache/2/yhpdlyc5vvdwkza0olml400b/52531702212017011451452.PDF.

[9] See the recently published edited collection *Animal Metropolis: Histories of Human-Animal Relations in Urban Canada*, eds. Joanna Dean, Darcy Ingram, and Christabelle Sethna (Calgary: University of Calgary Press, 2017).

[10] Sean Kheraj, "Urban Environments and the Animal Nuisance: Domestic Livestock Regulation in Nineteenth-Century Canadian Cities," *Urban History Review/Revue d'histoire urbaine* 44, no. 1–2 (Fall/Spring 2015/2016): 46.

[11] Sean Kheraj, "Living and Working with Domestic Animals in Nineteenth-Century Toronto," in *Urban Explorations: Environmental Histories of the Toronto Region*, ed. L. Anders Sandberg, Stephen Bocking, Colin Coates, and Ken Cruikshank (Hamilton: L.R. Wilson Institute for Canadian History, 2013), 129–30.

[12] *Annual Reports of the Chief of Police for Montreal* (Montreal: 1893), 22–23.

[13] "Pigs Continue to Roam the Streets," *Daily Free Press*, October 21, 1874, 3.

[14] "Pigs 'On the Loose'" *Toronto Mail*, October 21, 1872, 4.

[15] Sean Kheraj, "Animals and Urban Environments: Managing Domestic Animals in Nineteenth-Century Winnipeg," in *Eco-Cultural Networks and the British Empire: New Views on Environmental History*, eds. James Beattie, Edward Melillo, and Emily O'Gorman (London: Bloomsbury, 2015), 280–81.

[16] "Detailed Statement of the Receipts and Expenditures on Account of the City of Toronto," *Appendix to City of Toronto Council Minutes*, 1884.

[17] "City Items," *Montreal Daily Witness*, September 24, 1874, 3.

[18] Kheraj, "Animals and Urban Environments," 276.

[19] *Annual Reports of the Chief of Police for Montreal* (Montreal: 1889), 11.

[20] "Recorder's Court," *Montreal Herald*, July 7, 1865, 2.

[21] Jennifer Bonnell, *Reclaiming the Don: An Environmental History of Toronto's Don River Valley* (Toronto: University of Toronto Press, 2014), 40–43.

[22] City of Vancouver Archives, Bylaw no. 7, March 7, 1887.

[23] City of Vancouver Archives, City Council Minutes, MCR 1-1, 23 August 1886; Health Committee Minutes, MCR 2-43, 31 January 1887.

[24] *Census of Canada, 1901*, vol. 1 (Ottawa, 1903), 22.

[25] Colin S. Campbell, "The Stampede: Cowtown's Sacred Cow," in Chuck Reasons, ed., *Stampede City: Power and Politics in the West* (Toronto: Between the Lines, 1984), 103.

[26] "Old Spirit," *The Albertan*, July 13, 1923; Hugh A. Dempsey, *Calgary: Spirit of the West* (Calgary: Glenbow and Saskatoon: Fifth House, 1994), 1.

[27] Donna Livingstone, *Cowboy Spirit: Guy Weadick and the Calgary Stampede* (Vancouver: Greystone, 1996), 68.

[28] Guy Weadick to J. A. Shoemaker, July 25, 1912, Calgary Exhibition & Stampede correspondence, 1912–1953, Weadick Fonds, Glenbow Archives, Calgary, Alberta (hereafter GA).

[29] Indian Agent (name illegible) to Guy Weadick, July 26, 1912, Weadick Fonds, GA.

[30] "List of Bucking Horses—1926 Stampede," "List of Stock Delivered to Clem Gardiner July 18, 1927," "List of Horses Purchases by Calgary Exhibition Co.," "Bucking Horse List 1927 Stampede," and "Bucking Horses 1927," series 7, Events Records 1927, M-2160-89, Stampede Fonds, GA.

[31] Clem Gardiner to Guy Weadick, July 8, 1927, series 7, Events Records 1927, M-2160-89, Stampede Fonds, GA.

[32] "1927 Bucking Horses List Office Copy," series 7, Events Records 1927, M-2160-89, Stampede Fonds, GA.

[33] "1929 Bucking Horses List," series 7, Events Records 1927, M-2160-91(a), Stampede Fonds, GA.

[34] Donald G. Weatherell, "Making Tradition: The Calgary Stampede, 1912–1939," in *Icon, Brand, Myth: The Calgary Stampede*, ed. Max Foran (Edmonton: Athabasca University Press, 2008), 26–28.

[35] Sampling from 1927–1930 horse lists, events records, and correspondence, series 5, M-2160-89 to 98, Stampede Fonds, GA.

[36] "List of Stock Delivered to Clem Gardiner July 18, 1927," series 7, Events Records 1927, M-2160-89, Stampede Fonds, GA.

[37] Dick Cosgrove to Guy Weadick, May 24, 1930, series 7, General Correspondence A–H 1930, M-2160-98, Stampede Fonds, GA.

[38] Guy Weadick to Dick Cosgrove, May 30, 1930, series 7, General Correspondence A–H 1930, M-2160-98, Stampede Fonds, GA.

[39] "List of Bucking Horses Owned by Calgary Exhibition Assoc. June 27, 1930," series 7, Events Records, 1930, M-2160-97, Stampede Fonds, GA.

[40] In 1930, Greasy Sal was still owned by Exhibition Co., delivered to manager Dick Cosgrove: "Horses Delivered to Dick Cosgrove," series 7, Events Records, 1930, M-2160-97, Stampede Fonds; but not on Events Records for 1930 or 1931: "Bucking Horses Calgary Stampede 1930," "Mr. Dillon's Bucking Horse List 1930," "Office Copy Bucking Horse List Stampede 1931," series 7, Events Records 1931, M-2160-97 and M-2160-101, Stampede Fonds, GA.

[41] Clay McShane and Joel A. Tarr, *The Horse in the City: Living Machines in the Nineteenth Century* (Baltimore: Johns Hopkins University Press, 2007), 34.

[42] Keith Thomas, *Man and the Natural World: Changing Attitudes in England, 1500–1800* (New York: Vintage, 1983), 17–50, 242–303.

[43] Peterson and Fisher detailed their journey in *Wild America* (Boston: Houghton Mifflin, 1955).

⁴⁴ A robin that lacks some pigments, including melanin. As a result, its colour will appear muted.

⁴⁵ For more information, please visit the website of Aspire Food Group: http://www.aspirefg.com/about-us/.

⁴⁶ *Animal Studies Journal* 5(1) (2016). Special issue: Insects.

⁴⁷ For more information, please visit: http://www.cbc.ca/news/technology/meet-schmeat-lab-grown-meat-hits-the-grill-this-month-1.1343013.

⁴⁸ Scientific studies of evolutionary organic biology have recently found evidence for the "expensive tissue hypothesis"—the theory associating brain growth with expensive tissue meals such as meat (Tsuboi et al.).

⁴⁹ For more information, please visit: http://arts.ucalgary.ca/cih/who-we-are.

⁵⁰ For more information, visit the event's blog: http://arts.ucalgary.ca/cih/blog-posts/lunch-and-city.

⁵¹ For more information, see: https://www.soylent.com/.

⁵² The full plan is available online at http://www.calgary.ca/CSPS/Parks/Documents/Planning-and-Operations/BiodiverCity-strategic-plan.pdf.

⁵³ See http://www.lisabrawn.com/index.php/blog/item/helios.

contributors

Shelley M. Alexander is a professor in the Department of Geography at the University of Calgary. She has over twenty-five years' experience studying wild canid conservation, specifically wolves and coyotes. Shelley oversees the Canid Lab (www.ucalgary.ca/canid-lab), where her team practices Compassionate Conservation, using only non-invasive methods in wildlife research. Shelley is an established researcher in Animal Geography, Geospatial Analysis, Human Dimensions of Wildlife, and Road Ecology.

Lisa Brawn is a Calgary-based artist whose woodcuts have been exhibited in galleries across North America.

Kimberley Cooper has been dancing and making dance for most of her life. She is currently the Artistic Director of Decidedly Jazz Danceworks, which was founded in 1984 with a mission to preserve, promote, and evolve jazz dance.

Jim Ellis is director of the Calgary Institute for the Humanities, and a professor of English at the University of Calgary. He is the author of *Sexuality and Citizenship* (University of Toronto Press, 2003) and *Derek Jarman's Angelic Conversations* (Minnesota University Press, 2009), as well as other works on film, art, and literature.

Mohammad Sadeghi Esfahlani is a project manager for the Calgary Institute for the Humanities and a PhD Candidate in the Department of Communication, Media, and Film at the University of Calgary. His research interests include new social movements, social innovation, and energy systems transformation. His dissertation unravels the social dynamics of Germany's turn toward renewable energy sources ("Energiewende").

Paul Hardy is an internationally recognized fashion designer.

Andrea Hunt is the executive director at the Calgary Wildlife Rehabilitation Society. Andrea brings an eclectic skill set to her role as executive director, having previously worked with child protective services, managing a software development and media company, and maintaining a successful independent music career.

Sean Kheraj is an associate professor of Canadian and environmental history at York University. He is the director and editor-in-chief of the Network in Canadian History and Environment (NiCHE), where he produces Nature's Past: Canadian Environmental History Podcast. He is also the author of *Inventing Stanley Park: An Environmental History.*

Melanie Kjorlien is the VP Access, Collections and Exhibitions, at the Glenbow Museum in Calgary.

Maureen Luchsinger is the Education Coordinator and **Laura Griffin** is the Educational Interpreter at the Ann and Sandy Cross Conservation Area (ASCCA). They have taught youth from pre-school to university in Calgary and the surrounding area. They are passionate about conservation education to inspire youth to make connections that develop a love of the natural environment.

Jenna McFarland is the Animal Care Operations Manager at the Calgary Wildlife Re habilitation Society. As a zoologist and veterinary technologist she brings to CWRS a range of expertise from animal health, to nutrition, behaviour, and enrichment.

Susan Nance is a historian of communication and live performance in the US. She is currently working on a new book, *Born to Buck: Rodeo, Animals and the Myths of the West*. She is associate professor at the University of Guelph in Ontario and the author of various works, including *Entertaining Elephants: Animal Agency and the Business of the American Circus* (Johns Hopkins University Press, 2013).

One Yellow Rabbit Performance Theatre was founded in Calgary in 1982. *Calgary, I Love You, but You're Killing Me* premiered at their 30th High Performance Rodeo in 2016, featuring music and lyrics by Blake Brooker and David Rhymer, with additional music, lyrics and text by Denise Clarke, Andy Curtis, Kris Demeanor, Karen Hines, Michelle Kennedy, Jonathan Lewis, Jamie Tognazzini and Dewi Wood. The production was staged by Denise Clarke and performed by Denise Clarke, Andy Curtis, Karen Hines and Jamie Tognazzini.

Angela Waldie teaches at Mount Royal University. She completed her PhD at the University of Calgary, where her research focused on species endangerment and extinction in literature. She is currently writing her first poetry collection, entitled *A Single Syllable of Wild*, which explores wildlife conservation practices in the Canadian Rocky Mountain Parks.